Words for the Journey for Teens

Ten-Minute Prayer Services for Schools

Lisa Freemantle, Les Miller and Melinda Rapallo-Ferrara

NOVALIS

© 2011 Novalis Publishing Inc.

Cover: Blaine Herrmann
Cover artwork: Lynne McIlvride Evans (www.mcilvride-evans.com)
Layout: Audrey Wells

Published by Novalis

10 Lower Spadina Avenue, Suite 400
Toronto, Ontario, Canada
M5V 2Z2

Head Office
4475 Frontenac Street
Montréal, Québec, Canada
H2H 2S2

www.novalis.ca

Cataloguing in Publication is available from Library and Archives Canada.

Printed in Canada.

We acknowledge the financial support of the Government of Canada through the Canada Book Fund for business development activities.

5   4   3   2   1   15   14   13   12   11

Acknowledgements

We owe our deepest gratitude to our beloved spouses and children for their endless patience and support while we worked to create these prayer services. We also wish to extend our appreciation to our colleagues from the York Catholic District School Board and the Ontario educational community, and to Joe Sinasac, Grace Deutsch, Lauretta Santarossa, Anne Louise Mahoney and Dayle Furlong at Novalis.
May they always journey with faith, compassion and love.

This book is dedicated to all those who help to nurture
the faith life of young adults.

Contents

Introduction

Words for the Journey for Teens is an original collection of 60 ready-to-use prayer services that encompass liturgical as well as secular themes. The prayers in this book are meant for use by Catholic secondary school students.

For every student attending a Catholic high school, prayer nurtures their development as whole Christians and is thus rooted in the curriculum. These students are on the cusp of adulthood. They have left childhood behind and are beginning to accept new responsibilities: learning to drive, choosing a career path, working at a part-time job. At the end of their high school years, students will enter the workforce full-time or go to college or university. It is not surprising that they are filled with questions, doubts and mixed feelings at this time in their lives. They question the world and their place in it. They want to know who they are and what their contributions will be. They want to fit in with their peers. They ask many questions about their faith and may at times feel like walking away from it. This is a challenging time, and some students (and their teachers and parents!) may feel uncomfortable as students find their way, but it is also an exciting stepping stone to adulthood.

The prayers in *Words for the Journey for Teens* offer one way to help high school students to praise, thank and talk to God on their own terms, to ask for forgiveness, and to explore their faith in a way that is meaningful to them and their friends. The prayer services are organized by month: each contains a scripture reading and various styles of prayer and reflection. An appendix lists simple ideas for planning and setting up each service.

Our world is filled with secular influences and distractions, changes and fads. That is why it is so important for teens to realize the constancy of faith. No matter what the latest fashions, or new technologies, or daily academic or social concerns that students encounter, God is ever present and always ready to listen, to love and to guide them in the midst of their growth, including their questions and their doubts.

How to Use This Book

Here are some things to keep in mind when you are preparing a prayer service:

- Read the suggestions for each prayer service that are found in the appendix.
- Choose readers ahead of time.
- Provide a copy of the prayer service to all participants. (Purchasers of the book may photocopy individual prayer services to be used by participants at the service.)
- Explain logistics for rituals (such as where or when to stand, or other actions) before you begin the prayer.
- Make the sign of the cross together at the beginning and at the end of each service (where you see a "+" in the text).
- Include the doxology (*For the kingdom, the power, and the glory are yours, now and for ever. Amen.*) at the end of the Lord's Prayer.
- Add live or recorded music to these prayer services if you wish.
- Where appropriate (particularly after a scripture reading), incorporate a few moments of silence into the prayer.

May the words within this book help to guide these adults of tomorrow towards a deeper understanding of their beliefs and accompany them a little way along their faith journey.

Blessings,
Lisa, Les and Melinda

September

Beginning the Journey: A New School Year

*I am the Lord your God ... who leads you
in the way you should go.*

(Isaiah 48:17)

Introduction

+ As we embark on a new school year, we are meeting new teachers, new students, new subjects and new challenges. This upcoming adventure can be overwhelming. It is comforting to know as we begin the journey that Jesus is our constant and devoted companion.

Scripture: Proverbs 4:10-27

Litany: Beginning the Journey

Jesus our guide and teacher,
we humbly ask your help
as we begin the journey.

All: Give us the anticipation
Of a fresh start, of new beginnings.

All: Give us the courage
To try new things, to join new clubs and teams.

All: Give us the imagination
To dream and envision what we might accomplish.

All: Give us the joy
Of re-establishing old friendships and making new connections.

All: Give us the patience
To become familiar with new routines and adjust to a new pace.

All: Give us the mindset
To accept new knowledge and be open to learning.

All: Give us the perseverance
To work to understand new materials and new subjects.

All: Give us the hope
To expect our best efforts and to plan for success.
May we grow in faith as we journey with you by our side.
Amen.

Closing Reflection

It is said that every journey begins with a single step. Let us take that first step with confidence, knowing that we do not travel alone. We know that Jesus watches over us and will give us what we need to persevere.
+ Amen.

Let Your Voice Be Heard

The voice of the Lord is full of majesty.
(Psalm 29:4)

Opening Prayer

+ Gracious God,
grant us the ease
to express ourselves honestly.
Help us to listen attentively.
Teach us to uphold the dignity of all.
Encourage us to share our ideas and opinions.
We ask this through Christ our Lord.
Amen.

Introduction

It's easy to let others speak for us. It may feel more comfortable to just listen to the contributions of others. But a vibrant home, school, church and community comes from sharing all ideas and opinions. Let your voice be heard!

Scripture: Romans 15:18-21

Litany: Let Your Voice Be Heard

Let us generously offer our contributions to our community.

All: Let your voice be heard at school.
In the classroom, in the cafeteria, in sports, in the clubs you join, on the teams you play, express yourself. Let your voice be heard!

All: Let your voice be heard at home.
At mealtimes, with family, with friends, in the morning, in the afternoon, in the evenings, share your feelings and daily experiences. Let your voice be heard!

All: Let your voice be heard at church.
As a lector, a musician, a singer in the choir, a leader in the children's liturgy, joyfully express your faith. Let your voice be heard!

All: Let your voice be heard in the community.
Contribute your gifts, your time, your energy and your creativity. Let your voice be heard!

All: Let your voice be heard…
In your laughter, your tears, your frustrations, your opinions, your feelings, your prayers. Let your voice be heard!
Amen.

Reflection

Let your voice be heard. Too often we worry about what others may think. We may believe that our contributions are not important or popular. Let others know what you're thinking. Only then, with all the information available, can decisions be made. Don't just stand by. Let your voice be heard!

Closing Prayer

Loving God,
we ask for your blessing.
Give us the confidence to express our thoughts and feelings with caring and compassion.
Encourage us to make positive contributions to our community.
Show us how to listen to opposing ideas calmly, respectful of the dignity of all.
Teach us to be tactful and courteous.
We ask this through Jesus Christ your Son.
+ **Amen.**

Take Heart, Take Courage

Be strong, and let your heart take courage.
(Psalm 31:24)

Introduction

Autumn has arrived. This season is a
time of change, transition and retreat.
The bright, sunny days of summer are now
a distant memory. Dark falls earlier and
earlier, and there is a chill in the air. Our
lives change like the seasons do. At times,
our days are "sunny" and we feel brave,
confident, bold and unwavering. At other
times, there is darkness. We feel insecure,
anxious and afraid. We look to God for the
courage to renew our spirits so that we feel
the light of God's presence once again.

Opening Prayer

+ Ever-loving God,
be with us
as we place all that we are
in your hands.
Our struggles overwhelm us
and our efforts make us weak and tired.
Although darkness may fall upon us,
we look for the promise of a new dawn,
when the sun rises
and we are once again
blinded by your light and all its beauty.
Amen.

Scripture: Psalm 27:1-7, 13-14

Litany: Lord, Give Us Courage

When our journey is dark and lonely,
All: Lord, give us courage.

When we are driven by despair,
All: Lord, give us courage.

When temptation calls us,
All: Lord, give us courage.

When the right choice
isn't always the popular choice,
All: Lord, give us courage.

When our bodies are weak and tired,
All: Lord, give us courage.

When our hearts are heavy with burdens,
All: Lord, give us courage.

Help us to do your will always.
All: Lord, give us courage.
Amen.

Closing Prayer

Gracious, loving God,
we come to you
during difficult times.
We ask you to be near us
as we move into the unknown.
Protect us
and be our refuge.
Guide us
and lead us as you have promised.
Shelter us
for we are your servants.
Surround us
in your constant love.
+ **Amen.**

The Light of Insight

By wisdom a house is built, and by understanding it is established; by knowledge the rooms are filled with all precious and pleasant riches.
(Proverbs 24:3-4)

Opening Prayer

+ Spirit of Wisdom,
guide us in our learning this year.
May our curiosity lead to questions.
May our questions lead to understanding.
May our understanding reach beyond
insight into wise actions.
May our wise actions all be done
in your name and in your service.
Open our minds and hearts
as we listen to your word.
Be light for our journey,
bringing comfort and guidance.
Grant us the vision to see
with the eyes of faith and love.
Let the Spirit of insight lead us
and bring us closer to you.
Amen.

Scripture: Mark 10:46-52

Prayer of Light

Loving God,
we stand up to claim our own dignity.
We take heart and allow you to carry us forward.
We listen to your call in prayer and worship.
Flood our blindness with your light.
Shine hope onto our daily paths.
Listen to our deepest longings.
Give us the courage to speak of your love
and the strength to bring your peace and
justice into our world.

Litany: Let Us Bring Light to the World

Lord of all ages,
you are the light of the world.
Help us to reflect your light wherever we go.

To the people of Israel, you were a pillar of
fire and a light to their path.
All: Let us bring light to the world.

To Bartimaeus, you brought the light
of wisdom.
All: Let us bring light to the world.

To the people on the mountain, you spoke
of letting one's light shine before all.
All: Let us bring light to the world.

To your disciples, you taught that you are
the light of the world.
All: Let us bring light to the world.
Amen.

Closing Prayer

God of light,
shine on us this year.
Make hidden things visible to us
in the light of your love.
Bring brightness into the dark corners
of our lives.
May that light reflect in our hearts,
bringing hope and joy to our friends and
family.
May that light reflect in our minds,
turning our experiences into deep wisdom
and loving action.
We ask for these blessings
in your holy name.
+ Amen.

Leadership Matters: Student Government

Happy are those who observe justice,
who do righteousness at all times.

(*Psalm* 106:3)

Introduction

+ Leading a body of students is an important and often daunting task. Student leaders need focus, dedication and wisdom to inspire confidence in those they represent and be able to exercise control and set limits. They must be able to represent the views of the student body as best they can and to steer the affairs of the student body in a direction that benefits the majority. Above all, to be true leaders, they must remember that they are servants of those for whom they speak.

Jesus is our model of true leadership. It is with his guidance that we can learn to become effective, efficient and wise leaders in our schools.

Scripture: John 13:3-10

Reflection: Nine Principles of Leadership

No true leader can speak for all.
Leading is not imposing one's opinion on others. Rather, it is consulting with others to carefully meld the shared experiences and opinions to reach peaceful resolutions. Let us pray for the wisdom of our leaders to openly confer with others around them for advice and counsel.
All: O Lord, wisest of leaders, hear our prayer.

No true leader works alone.
Leading is not doing everything on one's own. It is the careful delegation of tasks that are suited to those who are given the assignment. Let us pray for the wisdom of our leaders to judiciously entrust and designate assignments and duties to those around them who are capable.
All: O Lord, wisest of leaders, hear our prayer.

No true human leader is infallible.
Leading is not being perfect in every way. It is learning from your mistakes and growing from the knowledge you gain from them. Let us pray for the wisdom of our leaders to gain new insight through experience.
All: O Lord, wisest of leaders, hear our prayer.

No true leader is belligerent, aggressive or confrontational.
Leading is not being the loudest and most strident, expecting all to follow. It is the careful picking out of the pathway using the experience of those who have gone before. Let us pray for the wisdom of our leaders to exert in a gentle way the influence and authority that their position affords over others, offering firm guidance rather than stringent rule.
All: O Lord, wisest of leaders, hear our prayer.

No true leader seeks abundance glory for themselves.
Leading is not for self-gratification. It is the enjoyment and rejoicing in the little successes of the entire group and the

striving to bring to fruition the promise of all. Let us pray for the wisdom of our leaders to look outward rather than inward to mark the success of the group.

All: O Lord, wisest of leaders, hear our prayer.

No true leader looks only forwards. Leading is not just facing where you are going. It is also examining where you have come from, since past experiences can teach you much about where you need to be. Let us pray for the wisdom of our leaders to take a look at the whole picture to gain perspective, encompassing the past, the present, and future hopes.

All: O Lord, wisest of leaders, hear our prayer.

No true leader is impulsive, acting without thinking first. Leading is not headlong decision making. It is action after careful thought and collaboration with those you represent. Let us pray for the wisdom of our leaders to think before acting to ensure progress in the right direction, even if it is just baby steps.

All: O Lord, wisest of leaders, hear our prayer.

No true leader is above the law. Leading is not just making rules for others to follow. It is also living within the set policies and limits themselves. Let us pray for the wisdom of our leaders to live within the rules they make.

All: O Lord, wisest of leaders, hear our prayer.

No true leader is wavering. Leading is not endless equivocating. It is finally making the difficult decisions and then sticking to it. Let us pray for the wisdom of our leaders to make the difficult decisions.

All: O Lord, wisest of leaders, hear our prayer.

Let us pray to our wisest leader, Jesus Christ, with the words he has taught us.
Our Father…

Closing Prayer

God of wisdom,
let us pray for those in student government,
that they may lead with hearts open to God,
eyes open to the past, present and future,
ears open to the voices and opinions of others,
minds open to compromise, and
the willingness to stay the course
when decisions have been reached.
We ask this through your Son our leader,
Jesus Christ.
+ Amen.

Who Is Jesus?

"But who do you say that I am?"
(*Mark* 8:29)

Invitation to Prayer

+ Jesus is our King, our Saviour and the Son of God. But unlike most kings, he did not live in a castle, wear rich robes or employ servants. Unlike many modern-day celebrities, Jesus never asked for fame or fortune. As Son of the Most High, he does not look down on us with arrogance and coldness, but with love and friendship. So who is Jesus, anyway? If we were to walk down the street and bump into him, would we recognize him?

Scripture: John 6:35-40

Litany: Who Is Jesus?

Jesus is our king, yet
he didn't live in a luxurious palace.
All: He walked among the poor, in leper colonies and spent time in the wilderness.

He didn't wear fancy clothing and designer shoes.
All: He wore plain robes and simple sandals.

He didn't wear a golden jewelled crown.
All: He was crowned with a ring of thorns.

He didn't ask us to bow before him and serve him.
All: He lived to serve others and washed the feet of his friends.

Jesus was a teacher, yet
he didn't take attendance.
All: He has called each of us by name.

He didn't assign homework.
All: He assigned us to feed the hungry, clothe the naked and care for the sick.

He didn't teach in a classroom.
All: He taught from a mountain, beneath olive trees and in a fishing boat.

He didn't ask questions on exams.
All: He looked for answers within the hearts of those who followed him.

Jesus was a leader of a group, yet
he didn't act superior.
All: He spoke to all as equals, as friends.

He didn't lead his disciples to become famous.
All: He led them to understand his Father's kingdom.

He didn't select only the best-looking people to be on his team of followers.
All: He chose those with humble hearts who would form a team of compassion and faith.

He didn't walk before them, leaving them to follow behind.
All: He walked *with* them every day.

Jesus is the Lord and is all powerful, yet
he didn't boast about his exploits.
All: He asked those he helped to tell no one.

He didn't charge money for his time.
All: He freely performed miracles to believers.

He didn't seek to help people who were wealthy, influential and popular.
All: He sought out sinners, the poor and the shunned people of society.

Who is Jesus?
Jesus is our king, yet he is humble.
Jesus is our teacher,
yet he is our friend.
Jesus is our leader,
yet he walks with us always.
Jesus is our Lord.
May we walk with Jesus at our side
all the days of our lives.
Amen.

Let us now pray in the words that Jesus
taught us:
Our Father …

Closing Prayer

God of power,
may we be ever blessed by Jesus,
our king and Saviour.
May we learn the lessons of life and love
from Jesus our teacher.
Help us to remember that we can talk to
him in prayer as our friend.
May we follow Jesus, our leader, and allow
him to accompany us in all we do.
May we praise Jesus the Lord.
+ Amen.

October

We Belong: School Teams and Clubs

See what love the Father has given us,
that we should be called children of God.

(*1 John* 3:1)

Opening Prayer

+ Loving God,
you know that everyone wants to belong,
for this makes us feel safe, secure and loved.
We are part of your family. We all belong.
Encourage us to promote teamwork
and pull together.
Guide us in active co-operation and sharing
of our gifts in your service.
For we are all part of something bigger
than any one of us.
We are the family of God.
Teach us that when we fail, everyone shares
in the misfortune.
And when we succeed, everyone rejoices.
Help us discover that we all belong.
Amen.

Scripture: 1 John 2:12-14

Litany: We All Belong

Teams and clubs operate best when all the members collaborate and work towards a common goal.

All: Teach us, Jesus, that when everyone pulls together in the same direction, all benefit, for we all belong.

Sometimes the group fails to reach the goals that have been set. We need to stick together and offer one another emotional and moral support. These are the moments when we grow the most.

All: Teach us, Jesus, to join in moments of failure and to not assign all the blame to others, for none of us is perfect and all of us belong.

Sometimes everything goes right. Goals are not only met but surpassed. We need to remember the happiness and to include all in the sharing of the glory, no matter what their contribution.

All: Teach us, Jesus, to join in moments of rejoicing and not to take all the credit, for we all belong.

Every member offers their best. Each has different gifts. Help us to recognize the merits of each offering and to treat all contributions with respect.

All: Teach us, Jesus, to respect everyone who contributes to the team – coaches, players, teachers, chaplain, friends, parents and administrators – for all have an important role to play and all belong.
Amen.

Closing Prayer

God our Father,
help us to foster collaboration among members,
enhance empathy for others,
recognize the gifts that people offer,
and join times of rejoicing and times of failure.
We are part of something bigger than any of us.
We are members of the family of God
and we belong.
We ask this through your Son, Jesus.
+ Amen.

Being Thankful

Give thanks in all circumstances.
(1 Thessalonians 5:18)

Introduction

+ Generous God,
open our eyes so that we may recognize the
angels in our lives:
those who work behind the scenes,
those who help without expecting credit,
and those who freely offer so much of their
time and so generously of their gifts.
Open our ears so that we may hear the
grateful thanks of others
and respond with humble hearts.
Above all, open our hearts so that we always
remember to give thanks to you
for the gift of life.
Help us always to express our gratitude:
in our prayers, in our hearts,
in our actions and in our words.
We ask this through your Son, Jesus Christ,
our Lord.
Amen.

Scripture: Psalm 107:1, 8-9, 15-16, 31-32

Responsorial Prayer:
We Are Thankful, O Lord

The response is: **We are thankful, O Lord.**
For your Son Jesus Christ, our Saviour, who
is our guide in all we do. **R.**
For the opportunity to pray and grow
together as a community. **R.**
For the chance afforded to each of us to get
an education. **R.**
For the numerous choices of future jobs and
vocations. **R.**

For the unexpected moments of grace in our
lives. **R.**
For all the gifts we can share with others. **R.**
For the times we are of help to the stranger. **R.**
For time spent with our friends and family. **R.**
For time to rejoice when things go well. **R.**
For the ability to pray when life is awry. **R.**
For our teachers and administrators. **R.**
For our priests and chaplains. **R.**
For the comfort of the mundane. **R.**
For normality in times of chaos. **R.**
For music, dance and song. **R.**
For life that surrounds us. **R.**
For good food to eat. **R.**
For the bread of life. **R.**
For celebration. **R.**
For friendships. **R.**
For our homes. **R.**
For the world. **R.**
For prayer. **R.**
For peace. **R.**
For hope. **R.**
For faith. **R.**
For love. **R.**
For joy. **R.**
For all. **R.**
Amen.

Closing Prayer

Gracious God,
you are always with us in all we do.
You guide and watch over us as we grow.
Teach us to always show
our deepest appreciation to you,
who have given us life
and the opportunity to share it.
May we have ever thankful hearts.
+ Amen.

Let the Light Shine

In your light we see light.

(Psalm 36:9)

Invitation to Prayer

+ Each of us has a light that shines within us.
For some it shines brightly.
For some it is an intermittent brightness.
And for others the light barely flickers.
Don't be afraid to let the light of God
shine within you.

Scripture: Matthew 5:14-16

Litany: Let the Light Shine

All: Let the light shine
Through our actions; let it reflect our hearts,
our meaning, our decisiveness.

All: Let the light shine
Through our prayer; let it bring clear vision
to our thoughts and lighten any burdens we
carry in our hearts.

All: Let the light shine
Through our studies; let it spark our
inquisitiveness and bring enlightenment and
knowledge to our work.

All: Let the light shine
Through our sports and club activities;
let its glow become brighter in the new
abilities and victories we achieve
and sustain us when we face
disappointments and challenges.

All: Let the light shine
Through our daily activities; let it spark us
from the mundane and routine to recognize
the extraordinary in what appears to be
commonplace.

All: Let the light shine
Through our friends; let it thread its way
through shared experiences, casting no
shadows.

All: Let the light shine
Through our treatment of strangers;
let it warm our hearts to welcome the poor,
the lonely and the disadvantaged.

All: Let the light shine
Through our gifts; let it shimmer and glow
in shared benefits for all.

All: Let the light shine
Through our breath, our words, our eyes,
our hearts, our souls, our lives.

**All: Let the light of God shine through
each of us.
Amen.**

Closing Prayer

God of light,
you lead us from the darkness of our sin to
the light of your truth.
you convey us from the murkiness of the
unknown
to the bright knowledge of your kingdom.
You lead us in our lives through your Son,
Jesus.
Let your loving brilliance guide us on our
faith journeys,
warm our hearts to the lost and lonely,
and enlighten our minds to new
possibilities.
We ask this through your Son Jesus,
the True Light.
+ **Amen.**

The Virtue of Compassion

"It is more blessed to give than to receive."
(Acts 20:35)

Opening Prayer

+ Dear Lord,
you call us to open our hands and hearts
and help those in need.
Cleanse our spirits
so that we may feel renewed.
Fill our hearts with love,
light and purpose.
Calm our minds
so that we can see you in all those around us.
Help us to widen our circles
so that we may embrace those who need us
most.
Amen.

Scripture: James 2:14-17

Ritual

Let us take a few minutes of silence to
reflect on the virtue of compassion using
these guiding questions:

- How have you answered the call to
  act compassionately in the past?

  (Think of two examples.)

- When did you fail to act with
  compassion?

  (Think of two examples.)

- What can you do today to show your
  compassion for others?

  (Name two actions.)

Intercessions

Loving God, we offer you our prayers of
petition.
The response is: **Lord, open our
compassionate hearts.**

For world and local leaders, that their
decisions are guided by wisdom and
compassion.
All: Lord, open our compassionate hearts.

For those who are experiencing hardships in
their lives, that they get the help they need
so that their burdens become lighter.
All: Lord, open our compassionate hearts.

For the students and staff of our school
community, that we have the courage to be
beacons of hope and compassion in the lives
of others.
All: Lord, open our compassionate hearts.

Closing Prayer

Gracious and loving God,
you call us to see you
in all those around us.
May we be blessed with the love
you pour into our hearts,
for it is your love
that makes us whole.
Help us to turn our feelings of compassion
into truth and action.
Remind us, Lord,
that the love we give to others
is the greatest gift we can give to you.
+ **Amen.**

Called to Witness

"You did not choose me but I chose you."

(*John 15:16*)

Opening Prayer

+ Loving God,
you call us to walk the path of discipleship with you.
You call us to listen for your voice in scripture and in the world around us.
You call us to speak and live your word in our school and in our homes.
In times of hardship, comfort us.
In times of challenge, send us your wisdom.
In times of celebration, give us your joy.
Let peace rule in our hearts and govern our words and deeds.
Amen.

Scripture: Matthew 4:18-22

Jesus calls disciples to walk with him, to worship with him, to work with him and to give witness to his life. We are also called to walk, worship, work and witness with Christ.

Gospel Meditation: Call Me?

Call me?
You are calling me?
But you know I'm not as faith-filled as I could be.
Or as compassionate…
Or as wise.
I don't always do the right thing or know all the right things to do in church.
Am I really worthy of this call?
You say you believe in me.

I always thought it was supposed to be the other way around.
But you believe in me.
Well, that's the only way this is going to happen:
with you working with me all the way,
so I speak the way I know I should.
But there's more, you say…
I am to speak not just with words,
but with
kind arms reaching out,
wise feet taking me down proper paths,
compassionate eyes seeing through fear and loneliness,
forgiving ears listening beyond anger and pain.

Litany: The Witnesses

As witnesses, we walk in the company of saints and heroes of faith. We ask them to pray for us.
Mary, Mother of God, woman of wisdom and strength,
All: Pray for us.
St. Peter, imperfect yet devoted,
All: Pray for us.
St. Paul, reaching out beyond boundaries,
All: Pray for us.
St. Francis, reminding us to befriend nature,
All: Pray for us.
St. Vincent de Paul and Blessed Mother Teresa of Calcutta, caring for the poor,
All: Pray for us.
St. Thérèse of Lisieux, doing deeds with great love,
All: Pray for us.

Gandhi and Martin Luther King Jr., meeting
injustice with peaceful defiance,
All: Pray for us.
All good people who work to heal the earth,
resolving conflicts and removing injustices,
All: Pray for us.
Amen.

Closing Prayer

God of our pilgrim journey,
with gratitude we thank you and praise your
sacred presence with us, behind us
and in front of us.
May we always know that we walk in the
company of good people.
Sustain us and direct us when the work
wearies us.
Nurture us and comfort us when conflict
hurts us.
Bring hope and joy into our hearts so we
may show that gladness to others.
Bless us in our work,
Bless us in our rest,
Bless us in our prayer.
We ask for these graces in the name of Jesus
of Nazareth, the one who calls us.
+ Amen.

Living Our Faith

The Lord is my light and my salvation;
whom shall I fear?

(*Psalm 27:1*)

Opening Prayer

+ God of faith,
You ask us to live our lives as Jesus did.
May we answer your call to serve others
with open and loving hearts.
We ask this through your Son, Jesus Christ.
Amen.

Scripture: Hebrews 11:1- 7

Litany: Living Our Faith

In living our faith we are called to commit
our whole person – body, mind and soul –
as Christ asks. Let us follow his example and
use our intellect, our energies and our hearts
to make this world a better place for all.

Side A:
Let us use our eyes to view the world
through the lens of faith, for it is only
then that we see God's hands at work in us
every day.

Side B:
Let us use our ears to hear the spoken word
of God, for it is only then that we can listen
to God's call with open hearts.

Side A:
Let us use our voices to speak no evil, but
to spread the Good News, for it is only
then that our words can make a positive
difference in the lives of those around us.

Side B:
Let us use our arms to embrace the
marginalized, for it is only then that

our compassion can encircle the world,
promoting welcome and inclusion.

Side A:
Let us use our hands to touch the hearts
of those around us, for it is only then that
we can mould the world around us in the
image of Christ.

Side B:
Let us use our feet to walk the halls of
justice, for it is only then that we can
fully understand the tribulations that
some encounter and treat all people with
compassion and fairness.

Side A:
Let us use our hearts to love
unconditionally, for it is only then that we
can truly feel God's devotion for us, his
beloved children.

Side B:
Let us commit our minds to pray earnestly
to God, for it is only then that we can be
open to understanding his guidance and to
living out our faith fully.
All: Let us use our eyes, ears, voices, arms,
hands, feet, hearts and minds in God's
service as we live our faith.
Amen.

Closing Prayer

Faithful God,
let us answer your call to commit body and
soul to living our faith.
Grant us your guidance and support.
We ask this through Christ our Lord.
+ **Amen.**

November

Teach Us to Love: All Saints' Day

Above all, clothe yourselves with love,
which binds everything together
in perfect harmony.
(Colossians 3:14)

Introduction

+ The Church celebrates the feast days of numerous saints. These are people who in life were male or female, young or old, rich or poor, and from all parts of the world. Some are people from our distant past, while others are from our recent history. Saints will come from our futures, too. All who have become saints have lived their lives proclaiming the work of Christ. In doing so, they have shown their deep love to all around them through their deeds and their words. We are encouraged to emulate their example in our lives. May we, too, endeavour to become like the saints, carrying out the acts of Christ and living every day with love.

Scripture: 1 Corinthians 13:1-13

Litany: Teach Us to Love

Patron saints are special protectors chosen by the Church to guard over various areas of our lives. In the following litany, we pray to saints who protect us and our school.

St. Thomas Aquinas, *patron saint of Catholic schools,*
All: Teach us to love.
St. Cecilia, *patron saint of music,*
All: Teach us to love.
St. Genesius, *patron saint of theatre and actors,*
All: Teach us to love.

St. Sebastian, *patron saint of athletes,*
All: Teach us to love.
St. Albert the Great, *patron saint of science,*
All: Teach us to love.
St. Catherine of Bologna, *patron saint of artists,*
All: Teach us to love.
St. Vitus, *patron saint of dancers,*
All: Teach us to love.
St. Francis de Sales, *patron saint of writers and authors,*
All: Teach us to love.
St. John Chrysostom, *patron saint of orators,*
All: Teach us to love.
St. Francis of Assisi, *patron saint of ecologists (animals and the environment),*
All: Teach us to love.
St. Gabriel the Archangel, *patron saint of telecommunications,*
All: Teach us to love.
St. Martha, *patron saint of cooks,*
All: Teach us to love.
St. John Baptist de la Salle, *patron saint of teachers,*
All: Teach us to love.
St. Ferdinand III of Castile, *patron saint of administrators,*
All: Teach us to love.
St. Jerome, *patron saint of libraries and librarians,*
All: Teach us to love.
St. Ignatius of Loyola, *patron saint of retreats,*
All: Teach us to love.
St. John Vianney, *patron saint of priests,*
All: Teach us to love.
St. John of Capistrano, *patron saint of chaplains,*
All: Teach us to love.
And all the saints,
All: Teach us to love.
+ Amen.

We Look to You: All Souls' Day

*"They will hunger no more, and thirst no more ...
and God will wipe away every tear from their eyes."*
(Revelation 7:16-17)

Opening Prayer

+ God of comfort,
may our hearts be open
to your healing touch.
May our spirits be prepared to acknowledge
the glory of your heavenly kingdom.
We ask this through Jesus your Son and our
brother in love.
Amen.

Scripture: John 14:1-7

Litany: We Look to You

All: We look to you with praise
For the blessing of the lives of our departed
loved ones,
All: In praise
For opening your arms to receive our kin,
All: In praise
For the home of peace and love
in which they now reside,
All: In praise
For the welcome you give to all your
cherished children.

All: We look to you with hope
For healing amidst our sorrow for our loss,
All: With hope
For an abating of our mourning with the
knowledge that our loved ones rest in you,
All: With hope
For the promise of tomorrows without grief
and heartache,

All: With hope
For serenity that will return to our hearts in
your time.

All: We look to you in remembrance
Of the life of our loved ones,
All: In remembrance
Of their patience and strength,
All: In remembrance
Of their love and support,
All: In remembrance
Of their humour and companionship.

All: We look to you in thanksgiving
For our fond memories,
All: In thanksgiving
For the sharing of gifts,
All: In thanksgiving
For your everlasting love,
All: In thanksgiving
For the comfort you offer us.

God of comfort,
we look to you with praise, hope,
remembrance and thanksgiving.
May our souls be open vessels
into which you can pour your wisdom.
Amen.

Closing Prayer

Compassionate God,
may we open our hearts
to receive your blessing.
May we open our souls
to witness your grace.
May we open our lives
to welcome your love.
We ask this through your Son,
our companion, Jesus Christ.
+ Amen.

Turning the Wheels of Justice

Do justice.

(Micah 6:8)

Introduction

+ We are called to act justly in God's name. Fairness, equality, mercy, peace, generosity and compassion are qualities that Jesus epitomizes and we should emulate. Let us become a just people of Christ.
Amen.

Scripture: Luke 6:27-36

Prayer: Turn the Wheels of Justice

Leader: Let us turn the wheels of justice from all that is hurtful to all that speaks of God's love for us. This heavy wheel will become lighter when we all work together to turn in the same direction and we all agree to love.

Side A: Let us turn the wheels of justice
... from war to peace
... from inequality to fairness

Leader: And gain

Side A: Friendship from peace and tolerance from fairness.

Side B: Let us turn the wheels of justice
... from grief to joy
... from hatred to love

Leader: And gain

Side B: Elation from joy and loyalty from love.

Side A: Let us turn the wheels of justice
... from pain to comfort
... from despair to hope

Leader: And gain

Side A: Friendship from comfort and promise from hope.

Side B: Let us turn the wheels of justice
... from distrust to faithfulness
... from disparity to covenant

Leader: And gain

Side B: Mercy from faithfulness and faith from covenant.

Side A: Let us turn the wheels of justice
... from isolation to companionship
... from loneliness to familiarity

Leader: And gain

Side A: Warmth from companionship and kinship from familiarity.

Side B: Let us turn the wheels of justice
... from discrimination to compassion
... from rejection to acceptance

Leader: And gain

Side B: Generosity from compassion and peace from acceptance.

All: Let us turn the wheels of justice
... from false pride to true humility
... from unawareness to understanding

Leader: And gain

All: Grace from humility and wisdom from understanding.

Closing Prayer

God of justice,
may we bring peace, love, compassion, fairness and acceptance to all we meet.
We ask this through your Son, Jesus.
+ Amen.

All Are Welcome: Equality and Acceptance

*Do not neglect to show hospitality to strangers,
for by doing that some have entertained angels
without knowing it.*

(Hebrews 13:2)

Introduction

+ We are all different from one another. We look different. We have different abilities and character traits. The numerous combinations of these are what make our world dynamic and interesting. Yet, in spite of the countless variations, in the eyes of God we are all equal. There are no human superstars in the kingdom of heaven. God has no favourites. Everyone warrants the same love and support. No one is excluded, for God is devoted to all his children equally. We are also called to welcome everyone.

Scripture: Matthew 10:40-42

Litany: All Are Welcome in God's House

All are welcome, all are loved.
All are equal in God's house, for we are all the cherished children of God.

The old and the young;
the experienced and the novice:
**All: All are welcome, all are loved.
All are equal in God's house.**

The wealthy and the destitute;
the famous and the obscure:
**All: All are welcome, all are loved.
All are equal in God's house.**

The retained and the discarded;
the beautiful and the unattractive:

**All: All are welcome, all are loved.
All are equal in God's house.**

The interesting and the dry;
the kind and the unpleasant:
**All: All are welcome, all are loved.
All are equal in God's house.**

The outgoing and the timid;
the proud and the meek:
**All: All are welcome, all are loved.
All are equal in God's house.**

The lively and the lethargic;
the clever and the dull;
**All: All are welcome, all are loved.
All are equal in God's house.**

The cheerful and the sombre;
the friendly and the distant:
**All: All are welcome, all are loved.
All are equal in God's house.**

People of all creeds and cultures; men and women, youth and children:
**All: All are welcome, all are loved.
All are equal in God's house,
for we are all the cherished children of God.
Amen.**

Closing Prayer

Welcoming God,
may we accept and include all in our midst;
appreciate any differences;
welcome all, no matter their creed, colour, sex, age, race, intelligence or financial standing.
We ask this through your Son Jesus, our model, who receives all, loves all, embraces all.
+ Amen.

Instruments of Peace: Remembrance Day

Seek peace, and pursue it.
(Psalm 34:14)

Introduction

On Remembrance Day, we reflect upon those people whose lives have been changed by war and conflict. True happiness comes when we are at peace with ourselves and others. At this time, you are invited to reflect on your hopes for peace. Where are you longing for peace the most?

Opening Prayer

Loving God,
you call us to be members of one body,
united in peace.
Forgive us for our selfishness.
Help us to establish a peaceful world that is built upon justice and truth.
Guide us so we can solve our conflicts
with compassion and humility.
Remind us to make every effort
to do what leads to peace.
Amen.

Scripture: Isaiah 2:2-4

Litany: We Are Instruments of Peace

Jesus, you taught us how to love our neighbours.
All: **We are instruments of peace.**

Jesus, you taught us how to embrace the weak, the sick and the lonely.
All: **We are instruments of peace.**

Jesus, you sacrificed your life for others, so that we can live.
All: **We are instruments of peace.**

Jesus, you have shown the way to a peaceful world.
All: **We are instruments of peace.**

Jesus, help us to forgive those who have wronged us.
All: **We are instruments of peace.**

Jesus, help us to practise your teachings each and every day.
All: **We are instruments of peace.**
Amen.

Prayer for Justice and Peace

For two minutes, let us pray in silence. Let us keep in our thoughts and in our hearts those who have died in war and other conflicts around the world.

Ritual

Leader: Let us share a sign of peace with each other.
All exchange a sign of peace.

Closing Prayer

Dear Lord,
you sent us your only Son
to teach us how to live
peacefully and lovingly.
Help us to express a love for all humanity
as Jesus showed us.
May we use the life of Jesus
to remind us to
turn our hearts towards peace,
rejoice in our commonalities,
and embrace our differences.
Guide our steps
so we may live as instruments of peace.
+ Amen.

Healing a Broken World: Social Justice

We, who are many, are one body in Christ,
and individually we are members
one of another.

(Romans 12:5)

Opening Prayer

+ Gracious God,
strengthen us
through your Spirit.
Help us to do your work
through our hands.
Ground us with love
through the gift of your grace.
May Christ dwell in our hearts
through our living a life of service.
Amen.

Scripture: Romans 12:1-8, 10-15

Litany: Lord, Help Me to Live a Life of Love

Reader 1: Let us reflect on some examples from the life of Jesus that show us how we can bring healing to the world through service, peace, love and trust in the Lord.

Reader 2: Jesus, through your actions of healing the sick and the marginalized, you show us how to love those around us: not only our families and friends, but also people in our communities and around the world who may need our help. You teach us to love our neighbour as ourselves.
All: Lord, help me to live a life of love.

Reader 2: Jesus, on the night of the Last Supper, you washed the feet of the disciples.

You taught us the importance of living a life of service by washing one another's feet.
All: Lord, help me to live a life of service.

Reader 1: Jesus, you forgave Judas when he betrayed you. Through your teachings on forgiveness, you show us how we can instill peace in our hearts and between one another.
All: Lord, help me to live a life of peace.

Reader 2: Jesus, you performed many miracles during your time on earth. Through your actions, you show us that God loves us all.
All: Jesus, help me to live in your glory.

Readers 1 & 2: Jesus, through your actions here on earth, you teach us how we can do our part to heal our families, our communities, our nation, our world.
Amen.

Closing Prayer

Loving God,
you call us to help
heal our broken world.
You call us,
not as individuals,
but as a community,
as one body.
Help us to see your glory
in all those we meet.
Help us to turn your words
and your teachings into action.
May we be united in Jesus Christ.
+ Amen.

December

Advent 1: Waiting in Hope

*I will wait for the Lord ...
and I will hope in him.*

(Isaiah 8:17)

Introduction

+ In our Church, Advent is the time to slow down and wait with patience. Yet in today's culture, Advent is the time to hurry and get ready for Christmas. While it is important to us to be ready with gifts, we also need to be ready in our hearts to receive the greatest gift, the Infant Jesus. Let us answer the call to be patient and to wait as Mary waited, with serene and hopeful hearts.

Ritual: While the first Advent candle is being lit, read the following prayer:

As we light the first Advent candle,
we see God's light reflected from the past,
shaping our present and shining with hope
for the future.
Let us follow God's light of hope.
Amen.

Reading: Isaiah 9:2-4, 6-7

Litany: Hope

All: May we wait in hope
Leader: For a future when all share in Christ's vision of peace, where war-torn nations become friends, where strangers reach out to help their neighbours, where kindness abounds.

All: May we wait in hope
Leader: For a tomorrow filled with shining potential and a realization of dreams coming true for all, where no limitations exist for the ability to get an education, adequate clothing, food and water, and where dignity is shared by everyone.

All: May we wait in hope
Leader: For the coming of Emmanuel, God-with-us, who is our dearest hope for all great futures.

All: As we wait in hope,
Leader: Let us work towards peace in our world. Let us help the disadvantaged, the lonely and the sick in our own communities. Let us answer the call for hope through thoughtful action.

All: As we wait in hope,
Leader: Let us show respect to all people around us, both our near neighbours and those around the world.

All: As we wait in hope,
Leader: May we share the anticipation of this Advent season as we look to the birth of our Saviour, Jesus Christ.
Amen.

Closing Prayer

Hope-filled God,
may we pray with hope
for a future of brightness.
May we live up to the potential
you have set for us.
May we answer the call of hope.
We ask this through Jesus Christ our Lord.
+ **Amen.**

Advent 2: Waiting in Faith

*"Go, let it be done for you
according to your faith."*

(Matthew 8:13)

Introduction

+ In this culture of instant gratification,
instant communication and instant cash,
waiting is hard for us. Yet, during Advent,
we are called to be watchful and to patiently
await the coming of Christ the Redeemer.
Let us actively wait for him by inviting him
into our daily lives with prayer. It is then
that we will indeed see the Christ child with
the eyes of faith.

*Ritual: While the second Advent candle is being lit,
read the following prayer:*

The faith in the Good News that the early
Christians handed down to us gives us
strength.
Our complete trust in the light of God's
wisdom and truth today nourishes us.
And our belief in God's everlasting
confidence for our tomorrows sustains us.
Let us follow God's light of faith and hope.
Amen.

Scripture: Luke 1:26-38

Litany: Faith

All: May we wait in faith
Leader: For a time when all are true to their
commitment to their beliefs,
where they not only speak about their faith
but act on it as well.

All: May we wait in faith
Leader: For a future where all can trust
in the support of others, whether family
members, friends or strangers, in times of
joyful celebration and in times of pain and
sorrow.

All: May we wait in faith
Leader: For the coming of Jesus our king,
who is the truest sign of faith for us and for
all future generations.

All: As we wait in faith,
Leader: Let us open our hearts to the word
of God, allowing it to infuse our souls
and guide us in all our deliberations, our
decision making and our actions.

All: As we wait in faith,
Leader: Let us answer the call to be the
faithful eyes, feet and hands of God as
we help those who are in need, especially
during this Advent season.

All: As we wait in faith,
Leader: Let us look to the child Jesus with
faithful hearts. May we strengthen our
commitment to our faith as we share our
beliefs through our prayer, our words and
our actions, this Advent season and always.
Amen.

Closing Prayer

Faithful God,
may your word strengthen, nourish and
sustain us.
May we answer your call to truly live with
faith in all areas of our lives.
We ask this through Jesus Christ our Lord.
+ **Amen.**

Advent 3: Waiting in Joy

*"As soon as I heard the sound
of your greeting, the child in my womb
leaped for joy."*

(Luke 1:44)

Introduction

+ As we draw nearer to the celebration of the birth of Jesus, waiting becomes more difficult. We worry about getting everything done in time and done well: decorating, get-togethers, and gifts for those we love. While the decorations, gatherings and gifts help us to get ready outwardly, it is even more important to prepare spiritually. During the third week of Advent, we are called to spread the joy of God's love to all around us.

Ritual: While the third Advent candle is being lit, read the following prayer:

As we light the third Advent candle,
we think of the great joy of Mary,
who is awaiting the birth of her son.
May we also wait in joyful anticipation for his coming.
Let us follow God's light in joy, faith and hope.
Amen.

Scripture: Luke 1:46-55

Litany: Joy

All: May we wait in joy
Leader: For a future when all share in Christ's dream of everlasting peace for every soul on earth, no matter their station, education, age, sex, race, colour or religion.

All: May we wait in joy
Leader: For a world of tomorrow that is filled with the peace of shared self-worth, free from the worries of loneliness and exclusion.

All: May we wait in joy
Leader: For the coming of Jesus, the Prince of Peace, who brings us the deepest joy in our everyday lives and for all future generations.

All: As we wait in joy,
Leader: Let us find in our hearts the brightness of God's joy and share it with those around us.

All: As we wait in joy,
Leader: Let us be open to freely sharing our gifts and appreciating the talents and abilities that others share with us.

All: As we wait in joy,
Leader: Let us look to the coming of Emmanuel with joyful hearts and share that joy with others.
Amen.

Closing Prayer
Joyful God,
may our quiet smiles be a symbol of remembered joys.
May our delight be a sign of our elation today.
May our laughter be signs of mirthful anticipation this Advent and always.
We ask this through Jesus Christ our Lord.
+ Amen.

Advent 4: Waiting in Love

O give thanks to the God of heaven,
for his steadfast love endures forever.

(Psalm 136:26)

Introduction

+ The wait is almost over. Our preparations are almost complete. Now it is time to examine our hearts and to quietly listen to the voice of God. It is in the still moments that we can hear God's words most clearly. We are called to find moments of peace to praise God with love during this last week of Advent.

Ritual: While the fourth Advent candle is being lit, read the following prayer:

As we light the fourth Advent candle,
we can feel the light of God's love from the past,
brightly shining in our present and warming our future.
Let us follow God's light of hope, faith, joy and love.
Amen.

Scripture: Luke 1:39-45

Litany: Love

All: May we wait in love
Leader: For a time to come when all around the world share in the knowledge that we are the cherished children of God.

All: May we wait in love
Leader: For a future that is free from hatred, envy and greed and is filled instead with goodwill, generosity and abundant love.

All: May we wait in love
Leader: For the birth of our king, Jesus, who showers us, his cherished children, with love.

All: As we wait in love,
Leader: Let us answer God's call to love one another. Let us love others courageously, wholeheartedly and without reserve.

All: As we wait in love,
Leader: Let us show respect and caring to our neighbours and to strangers, love to our families and friends, and devotion to our God.

All: As we wait in love,
Leader: Let us look to the child Jesus with loving hearts. May we share in the anticipation of this Advent season as we look to the birth of our king and Saviour, Jesus Christ.
Amen.

Closing Prayer

Loving God,
we await the birth of your Son with love.
May we always praise you with adoration.
May you lead us to love others in your service.
We ask this through your Son, Jesus Christ.
+ **Amen.**

Gifts for the Season

Then, opening their treasure chests,
they offered him gifts of gold,
frankincense, and myrrh.

(Matthew 2:11)

Opening Prayer

+ God of Christmas promise,
still our busy lives,
open our frantic hearts,
make our world a fit place to receive the
Prince of Peace.
Bless our humble attempts to prepare for
Christ's birth
through acts of service and charity.
Bless those who receive these gifts;
may they bring joy in this season of hope.
Open our ears to hear your word,
lived in acts of justice and spoken in your
scriptures.
Amen.

Scripture: Matthew 25:31-46

Gospel Meditation:
Where Are They Now?

Where are they now?
The stranger, the naked, the sick, the
prisoner?
Are they in our school? In our community?
In our family?
Yes, they are.
I know this because I am all of these.
I'm a stranger and outsider at times.
Sometimes people just don't know me and
they reject me.
I stand naked and embarrassed when the
truth comes out and my vulnerability shows.

I am physically sick sometimes, but often
spiritually sick, when God seems far away.
I am imprisoned by my fear of being
rejected, unlovable.
If these figures are in me, I know they are in
others also.
So yes, they are here.
The good news is that Christ is there, too:
in our vulnerability and our shame,
in our loss and in our fears.
With Christ-like love we approach the
stranger, the naked, the sick and the
prisoner and welcome them home.

Litany: The Gifts

Dear Jesus,
we approach your manger this year
as the magi did two thousand years ago.
Like them, we bring gifts.
Not gold, frankincense or myrrh,
but things many people need this
Christmas.
Bless these gifts and treasure them.
You have given us so many spiritual gifts;
we know that we are in turn to give them to
others.
Gifts of forgiveness and mercy:
All: Lord Jesus, bless them.
Gifts of understanding and compassion:
All: Lord Jesus, bless them.
Gifts of wisdom and courage:
All: Lord Jesus, bless them.
Gifts of hope and joy:
All: Lord Jesus, bless them.
Gifts of faith and devotion:
All: Lord Jesus, bless them.

Gifts of justice and peace:
All: Lord Jesus, bless them.
Gifts of love:
All: Lord Jesus, bless them.
Amen.

Closing Prayer

Creator God, Prince of Peace, Spirit of Life,
bless all that we have to offer.
In this season when we ready ourselves to
celebrate the coming of Christ into the
world,
give us eyes to see you being born again and
again
in those who live on the edges of society.
Give us eyes to see you being born again
and again
in our families and friends.
Give us eyes to see you being born again
and again
in our own humble hearts.
We make this prayer in the name of Jesus
Christ our Lord.
+ Amen.

Christmas Blessings

"I have come as light into the world, so that everyone who believes in me should not remain in the darkness."

(John 12:46)

Introduction

+ The season of Christmas, when Christians around the world celebrate Jesus' birth, is fast approaching. The Gospel of Luke tells a story about a baby born to an ordinary woman, and laid in a manger, in a stable. "He was named Jesus, the name which the angel had given him before he had been conceived" (Luke 2:21). How are you preparing for this sacred time of year?

Opening Prayer

Dear God,
the Christmas season is almost upon us.
Help us to keep our hearts
focused on the true reason for our
celebrations:
the birth of your Son Jesus,
whose incarnation
is the miracle of all miracles.

Remind us, dear Lord,
amidst the busy-ness of Christmas,
amidst the lights, decorations and gift giving,
that there is good news to share:
the Messiah, named Jesus, is born.
Amen.

Scripture: Luke 2:1-20

A Shared Reading

Reader 1: Joseph went from the town of Nazareth in Galilee to the town of Bethlehem in Judea, the birthplace of King David. Joseph was there because he was a descendent of David. He went to register with Mary, who was promised in marriage to him. She was pregnant, and while they were in Bethlehem, the time came for her to have her baby.

Reader 2: She gave birth to her first son, wrapped him in cloths, and laid him in a manger – for there was no room for them to stay at the inn.

Reader 3: There were some shepherds in that part of the country who were spending the night in the fields, taking care of their flocks. An angel appeared to them, and the glory of the Lord shone over them. They were terribly afraid, but the angel said to them,

Reader 4: "Don't be afraid! I am here with good news for you, which will bring great joy to all people. This very day in David's town your Saviour was born – Christ the Lord! And this is what will prove it to you; you will find a baby wrapped in cloths and lying in a manger."

Reader 5: When the angels went away from them back into heaven, the shepherds said to one another,

Reader 1: "Let us go to Bethlehem and see this thing that has happened, which the Lord has told us."

Reader 2: So they hurried off. They found Mary and Joseph and saw the baby lying in the manger. When the shepherds saw him, they told Mary and Joseph what the angel had said about the child. All who heard it were amazed at what the shepherds said.

Reader 3: Mary remembered all these things and thought deeply about them.

Reader 4: The shepherds left, singing praises to God for all they had heard and seen. It had been just as the angel had told them.

Scripture Reflection

- How do you think Mary felt when she was told that she would give birth to the Son of God?

- Why do you think the Messiah was born in these humble surroundings rather than into a wealthy royal family?

- How do you think the shepherds felt after being visited by the angel?

Closing Prayer

Loving God,
you sent us your only Son,
who began life on earth
in the most humble of
surroundings – in a stable.

As we celebrate Christmas
with our friends and family,
we thank you
for the gifts that you have given to us,
to our families, to our friends.

Guide us so we may experience
the spirit of Christmas
not just during this season
but every day of the year.
+ Amen.

January

Nurturing the Soul

I can do all things through the Lord
who strengthens me.
(Philippians 4:13)

Invitation to Prayer

+ Let us begin with a moment of silence.
The Lord God helps us to settle our minds
and hearts and be still.

Opening Prayer

God of all eternity,
you teach us that the kingdom of God
is within each of us.
Our faith begins as a tiny seed,
and grows perfectly,
through living a life of service and
compassion.
Guide us so we can experience
the divinity within us.
Remind us to take time
to nurture our souls
so we may grow strong and steadfast
in your love.
We ask this through your Son
Jesus Christ our Lord.
Amen.

Scripture: Matthew 13:31-32

Litany

Lord, we ask you to help us nurture our
souls so that our spirits may rejoice in your
glory.
The response is: **Help us to cultivate the
kingdom of God within us.**

Through our faith, hope and love,
**All: Help us to cultivate the kingdom of
God within us.**

Through our prayers and petitions,
**All: Help us to cultivate the kingdom of
God within us.**

Through our most challenging moments,
**All: Help us to cultivate the kingdom of
God within us.**

Through our compassionate words and
service to others,
**All: Help us to cultivate the kingdom of
God within us.**

Through your loving Son,
**All: Help us to cultivate the kingdom of
God within us.**
Amen.

Closing Prayer

Loving God,
you call us to nurture the kingdom of God
within us,
to sow the seeds of faith in your fields
and nurture their growth.
May we always be mindful
of taking time to cultivate
the divine love within us
and expand our vision,
so that we may believe in those things
we cannot see,
but feel a deep trust in you.
Let us come to know the kingdom of God
just as Jesus sees it.
+ Amen.

Take Time to Pray

Be careful then how you live …
making the most of the time.
(Ephesians 5:15)

Invitation to Prayer

+ God has given each of us the gift of time.
We are called to use it wisely.
Often, we feel we don't have enough time.
We're rushed, stressed, late.
We're falling behind.

Take the time to pray.
and take the time for God.
Amen.

Scripture: Ecclesiastes 3:1-8

Litany: Take Time to Pray

In the midst of preparations and exams,
All: Take time to pray.
In the midst of friendships,
All: Take time to pray.
In the midst of family life,
All: Take time to pray.
In the midst of studies and classes,
All: Take time to pray.
In the midst of games and recreation,
All: Take time to pray.
In the midst of celebrations and joyfulness,
All: Take time to pray.
In the midst of sorrows and woes,
All: Take time to pray.
Amen.

Reflection: Time

Time can be saved and spent.
You can save time
by finding efficient ways to complete tasks.
You can spend time
on things you like to do.

Time can be taken and given.
You can take time
to do things correctly.
You can give time
by sharing your talents with others.

Time can be used wisely or wasted carelessly.
You can use time well
by planning carefully,
but you can waste time
by paying it no heed.

God has given each of us the gift of time.
We are called to use it wisely.

Once time is lost, it cannot be retrieved.
It is up to us to use this precious gift well.

For all time, God has loved us, loves us,
and will love us.
God always has been, always is,
and always will be there to guide us.
Let us now praise God by praying
the Glory Be:
All: Glory be to the Father,
and to the Son,
and to the Holy Spirit.
As it was in the beginning,
is now, and ever shall be,
world without end. Amen.

Closing Prayer

God of time,
teach us to use time wisely in your service.
May we grow in faith and love, in your time.
May we serve you and others, in your time.
May we grow in understanding of your ways,
in your time.
We ask this through Jesus Christ, our Lord.
+ Amen.

Opening the Lines of Communication

"Consider, and then we shall speak."
(Job 18:2)

Introduction

+ When we pray, no matter what our mood is, God listens to us and reads our hearts. There is no block to communication. God hears even the quietest whisper or tiniest thought. But with people, a breakdown in communication is not uncommon. At times this breakdown is due to malfunctioning technology, but even more often it is the spirit of those sending and receiving the message that isn't working well. For good communication, our hearts, minds and ears must be fully open and attuned. Whether the information transfer is oral or written or gestured, those dispatching and accepting the communications need to be both attentive and receptive. Only then can the lines of communication be totally unblocked. We ask God for the patience and skill to communicate clearly.

Scripture: James 3:2-5

Litany: Communication

Communication can be deterred by misunderstandings between the sender and the recipient. Let us break down the barriers to communication so we can together take down the walls of doubt and distrust and build bridges of faith and confidence within our communities.

All: God of harmony, soothe our souls and calm our hearts so that we may speak clearly and truly hear the words of others.

Communication can be blocked by hostility, anger or resentment.
When we are angry or annoyed, we can say or write things in the heat of the moment that do not truly represent what we intend. It is only when we cool down that we realize the damage we may have caused.

All: God of harmony, soothe our souls and calm our hearts so that we may speak clearly and truly hear the words of others.

Communication can be barred by antagonism, opposition or disagreement. It can be hard to communicate with someone when we disagree or are on opposite sides of an issue. At times, looking for healing and mending of our differences seems like an insurmountable obstacle. To open lines of communication, we must put ourselves in the shoes of our opponents and view the situation from their side to gain understanding.

All: God of harmony, soothe our souls and calm our hearts so that we may speak clearly and truly hear the words of others.

Communication can be impeded by inattention, distraction or apathy. At times we can be distracted by other things that we think are more important, and so don't pay full attention to some of the messages we are receiving. It is only when we truly stop to consider that the sender believes their message is relevant that we realize we should pay attention.

All: God of sincerity, open our minds to be receptive to those who wish to communicate with us so we may speak clearly and truly hear the words of others.

Communication can be obstructed by delivery of mixed messages by a third party. In some cases, when the personal touch would be much more effective, we delegate others to accept and reply to messages for us. But relying on a third party can often lead to misunderstandings and misinterpretations, and the original message can be lost.

All: God of sincerity, open our minds to be receptive to those who wish to communicate with us so that we may speak clearly and truly hear the words of others.

Communication can be hampered by emotional upheaval, grief or pain. Strong emotions such as despondency, dejection or mourning make it very difficult for people to share information clearly or efficiently. At these times we are called to show empathy and patience.

All: God of peace, grant us tolerance and compassion so that we may speak clearly and hear the words of others.

Communication can be hindered by incomplete or unfinished messages. Sometimes, when we are rushing or busy, we deliver only part of the message or don't listen carefully. This leads to incomplete understanding of the message. We need to slow down and be attentive, even when we are busy.

All: God of peace, grant us tolerance and compassion so that we may speak clearly and hear the words of others.

Glorious God, as we journey through life, teach us to better communicate as individuals and as a community so that together we can build close links of faith. **Amen.**

Closing Prayer

God our Father,
you hear all our prayers to you.
Whether we are angry or hurt,
unhappy or joyful,
asking for forgiveness
or asking for miracles,
there is no obstacle to our connecting
with you.
Help us to open the lines of communication
to others around us.
Teach us to be sincere and honest
in all our conversations.
We ask this through your Son Jesus Christ,
our brother and friend.
+ Amen.

Bridges and Walls

"I give you a new commandment, that you love one another. Just as I have loved you, you also should love one another."

(John 13:34)

Opening Prayer

+ God of unity,
help us to build bridges of compassion and understanding
where people are separated from each other
by fear and anger.
Help us to tear down walls of prejudice and hatred
that separate country from country,
community from community,
and citizen from citizen.
Teach us that to be a Christian is to be a bridge builder and a wall remover.
Open our ears to your call for unity and mutual respect.
Amen.

Scripture: Galatians 3:27-29

St. Paul calls for Christians to be united in our faith in God. If we are truly one, then there are no walls that divide us.

Bridges and Walls

Across streams, across meadows,
I walked far away from home
to live in a far-off land.
It was a terrible exile.
I wanted to return home, but I couldn't.
A war had made any journey hazardous.
Trees were cut down to create weapons.
Walls were built to protect property.

Gradually, peace came to the war-weary land.
After many years, it was time to return home:
to the place where I belonged,
to the place where I felt connected,
to the place where I truly belonged.
My path home was rutted by war machines and blocked by high walls.
The streams had become torrents,
the forests that had held the water were gone, and
water cascaded down the hillside,
making crossing dangerous.
A few of us walked together for companionship and safety.
We clambered over the walls,
helping each other.
We made our slippery crossing over dangerous rivers.
One more day and one more wall.
There we met an elderly woman
who had a stone in her hand.
Slowly, rock by rock, she was taking the wall down, opening up the path.
Later, at another crossing, we came across a young man dropping stones into the water.
He told us he was making a ford to make the crossing easier.
Around the campfire that evening,
we reflected on these two meetings.
As story wove into story, wisdom emerged.
And wisdom created a plan.
The next morning we formed a line, taking stones from the wall,
passing them down the line to the stream.
At the stream, we built a bridge from these stones.

In this way we made our journey safer and easier.
Those who followed took down more walls and built better bridges.
In this way, we helped each other to return to our true homes.

Litany: Building Bridges of Unity

Loving God,
bring unity into our divided lives.
Help us to build bridges of compassion
All: From walls of rejection.
Help us to build bridges of justice
All: From walls of greed.
Help us to build bridges of peace
All: From walls of destruction.
Help us to build bridges of understanding
All: From walls of bigotry.
Help us to build bridges of faith
All: From walls of doubt.
Help us to build bridges of hope
All: From walls of despair.
Help us to build bridges of love
All: From walls of fear.
Help us to build bridges of joy
All: From walls of sorrow.
Amen.

Closing Prayer

Loving God,
help us to be wall removers and bridge builders.
May there never be any walls between us.
May we always have your guidance in building bridges.
Bring us safely to our true home,
the place where we are truly ourselves:
at home with you.
We make this prayer in the name of Jesus.
+ Amen.

St. Thomas Aquinas: God Directs Our Lives

I am the first and I am the last;
besides me there is no god.

(Isaiah 44:6)

Introduction

+ St. Thomas is the patron saint of Catholic schools and students. Thomas was born to a wealthy Italian family around the year 1225. He was an intelligent but quiet boy. Because he was also large, he earned the nickname "Dumb Ox." It was clear very early on that God was calling Thomas to serve in the priesthood. His wealthy family lined up a prestigious position for him as abbot of a Benedictine monastery. But Thomas desperately wanted to become a simple Dominican priest and live out his days in poverty and prayer. His family disapproved. They locked him up in the family castle for a year, hoping to change his mind. But Thomas refused to be derailed from this course. He strongly believed that being a Dominican priest was what God intended for him. He finally realized his dream. During his life he was moved to write many books on Christianity. Today, Christian scholars have hailed his writings, including his *Summa Theologica*, as some of the most powerful and enlightened works on Christianity.

Scripture: 1 Thessalonians 5:12-24

Litany of St. Thomas

Leader: In Thomas' writings, he described the nature of God in five simple statements. Let us use these statements to guide our prayer today.

The First Statement

Leader: *"God is simple, without composition of parts, body matter or form."*

Reader 1: God will always be whole and perfect, and though our bodies will fail,

All: **God will always love us,
even in our frailty.
Praise be to God, who formed us and directs our lives.**

The Second Statement

Leader: *"God is perfect and lacks nothing."*

Reader 1: God is ever holy, ever blessed, ever present. Though we make mistakes and pray for forgiveness for our transgressions,

All: **God will always love us,
even with our imperfections.
Praise be to God, who formed us and directs our lives.**

The Third Statement

Leader: *"God is infinite. God has no physical, emotional or intellectual limits."*

Reader 1: God always was, is and ever shall be. There are no bounds to God's existence. Though our human condition is finite,

All: **God will always love us, even with our earthly limitations.
Praise be to God, who formed us and directs our lives.**

The Fourth Statement

Leader: *"God is immutable. No changes will ever alter the essence of God."*

Reader 1: God will always be the same. God is steadfast and permanent. Though our humanity dictates that we continually change and grow,

All: **God will always love us, even with our changing natures. Praise be to God, who formed us and directs our lives.**

The Fifth Statement

Leader: *"God is One. There is no other. The Trinity forms the essence of God."*

Reader 1: God exists in the perfect Trinity: God the Father, God the Son, and God the Holy Spirit. Though we will not fully appreciate the glory of the Trinity until we meet God face to face,

All: **God will always love us, even with our limited mortal vision. Praise be to God, who formed us and directs our lives.**

God is simple, perfect, infinite and immutable, and God is One. Praise be to God, who formed us and directs our lives. Amen.

Closing Prayer

God our strength,
help us to be more like St. Thomas,
who trusted in your wisdom and power
to direct his life.
Strengthen our faith.
Lead us to your truth.
Guide us to serve you with love.
We ask this through your Son, our Saviour,
Jesus Christ.
+ **Amen.**

Trials: Exam Time

*The Lord your God [is] ... testing you to know
what was in your heart, whether or not
you would keep his commandments.*
(Deuteronomy 8:2)

Opening Prayer

+ Compassionate God,
grant us clearness of mind,
strengthen our determination,
ease our anxieties,
and guide us to peace in you.
We ask this through your Son,
our companion on the journey,
Jesus Christ our Lord.
Amen.

Scripture: Matthew 5:3-11

Litany: Our Trials

All: **Our learning provides us with new
lessons.
Our intellect reveals our understanding.
Our studies open doors of opportunity.**
Leader: But our trials allow us to consolidate
our knowledge.

All: **Our skills incline us to future
vocations.
Our interests prompt our dreams.
Our hope propels us ever forward.**
Leader: But our trials reveal our true hearts.

All: **Our fears impede our progress.
Our doubts weaken our resolve.
Our misgivings lead to hesitation.**
Leader: But our trials make us spiritually
stronger.

All: **Our patience leads to fresh outcomes.
Our labour reaps its own rewards.
Our care leads to precision.**
Leader: But our trials root us in truth.

All: **Our memories view past assessments.
Our hearts revel in the successes of today.
Our prayers long for bright tomorrows.**
Leader: But our trials open our minds to
timeless possibilities.
O Lord our God,
help us find our way to you
through our trials.
Amen.

Closing Prayer

Loving God,
show us the way of truth and light.
May we approach the trials in our lives
with strength of heart, open minds,
fresh energy, and trust in your truth.
Help us to find peace in your presence,
clarity in your love
and faith in your glory.
We ask this through your Son Jesus Christ,
our teacher and guide.
+ Amen.

February

The Journey Continues

May you be prepared to endure everything
with patience, while joyfully
giving thanks to the Father.
(Colossians 1:11-12)

Opening Prayer

+ God of the journey,
as we continue through this year,
we ask that you
guide us in our works of peace and
compassion,
inspire us to use our gifts in your service
to the best of our abilities,
and empower us with inner strength to
persevere in all our endeavours.
We ask this through your Son Jesus,
our leader and teacher.
Amen.

Scripture: Ezekiel 36:26-28

Litany: Renew Us

Jesus our guide and teacher,
we continue our journey,
following in your footsteps.
Renew us today so that we may walk with
fresh hearts.

All: Renew our courage:
When we face new challenges, quell our
fears, our worries and our anxieties.

All: Renew our energies:
In our efforts every day, refresh our
enthusiasm, our vigour and our strength.

All: Renew our understanding:
Bolster our efforts for new learning, new
insight and new wisdom gained both in
and outside the classroom.

All: Renew our dreams:
In our innermost hearts, fuel our desires, our
ambitions and our aspirations.

All: Renew our faith:
When things go wrong, support us in our
disappointments, in our mistakes and in our
failures.

All: Renew our joy:
When we celebrate successes small and
large, rejoice in our achievements, our
accomplishments and our triumphs.

All: Renew our patience:
When we reach the goals we set, grant
us persistence to continue our efforts,
endurance to stay the course and tolerance
to accept challenges that come our way.

All: Renew our hope:
In peace and unity, hear our prayer for
justice, equality and harmony within our
schools, our homes and our communities.
Amen.

Closing Prayer

Jesus our companion,
we continue our journey
hand in hand with you,
treading softly through the unknown,
confidently through the familiar
and with anticipation towards the future.
+ Amen.

The Key to Wisdom

Wisdom is a reflection of eternal light,
a spotless mirror of the working of God,
and an image of his goodness.
(Wisdom of Solomon 7:26)

Introduction

+ Wisdom is the absolute comprehension of all past, present and future knowledge. It includes complete insight into the human condition. It is also the interpretation of information that isn't always immediately apparent to all. It is the utter understanding of all that was, is and shall be. Jesus is the key to wisdom. His knowledge spans all time and space.

Scripture: John 7:10-18

Litany: The Key to Wisdom

Jesus' disciples sat at his feet, listening to the wisdom of his parables and messages about salvation. Jesus, in his wisdom, gave his life for us that we might enter the kingdom of God and have eternal life. Jesus is the key. He has unlocked the door to salvation.
All: Jesus is the key to heaven.
Jesus is the key to wisdom.

All: Jesus is the key to wisdom of our present.
In our lives there are many things that we find important: final papers and exams, team tournaments and work schedules, socializing with friends, and family obligations. One of the most important things that can be forgotten in this shuffle is that Jesus walks with us in our busy-ness, every day. He is that vital element that brings wisdom and clarity to our lives. Jesus is the key. Without him, our lives have little order.
All: Jesus is the key to order.
Jesus is the key to wisdom.

All: Jesus is the key to wisdom of our future.
We often wonder: Where am I going? What will I be? Who will I meet? What will I do? Jesus is the key. He will never turn his back on you. He will always welcome you with open arms. Jesus is the answer, the solution, the remedy.
All: Jesus is the key to life.
Jesus is the key to wisdom.
Amen.

Let us pray the words that Jesus, our Lord of wisdom, taught us.
Our Father…

Closing Prayer

God of wisdom,
we know that Jesus is the key to wisdom.
He has unlocked the door to heaven.
He has given us insight through his teachings about your kingdom.
He is the answer to our prayers
and walks with us daily.
May we model our lives after his example,
and may this strengthen our faith
as we make our way to you.
+ Amen.

The True Model of Friendship

*A true friend sticks closer
than one's nearest kin.*

(Proverbs 18:24)

Introduction

+ Jesus is the model of true friendship. It is through his example that we know what it is to be true friends. Jesus was our first and closest friend, who willingly gave up his life for all of us. We thank God for giving us his Son, the model of the truest friendship.

Scripture: John 15:12-17

Litany: Friendship

Leader: Jesus is the true model of friendship and our best friend.

Side A: Friends are our healers.

*They cry with us when we mourn,
bolster us when we need confidence
and support us when we fall.*

Leader: Jesus is our healer,
mending us in our brokenness.

Side B: Friends are our mirrors.

We see ourselves reflected in their eyes, in their actions and in their hearts. Friends walk with us along our life's journey.

Leader: Jesus is our mirror, reflecting perfect love back to us.

Side A: Friends are our sounding boards. They allow us to speak our minds honestly and completely. They do not judge us.

Leader: Jesus is our sounding board, listening to our deepest secrets and readily accepting us for who we are.

Side B: Friends are our cheerleaders.

They compliment us when they see us happy. They rejoice with us when we celebrate.

Leader: Jesus is our cheerleader, delighting in our smallest successes.

*Side A: Friends are our microscopes.
They bring our lives into focus. They help us to see more clearly where we have come from, where we are and where we hope to go.*

Leader: Jesus is our microscope, knowing us inside and out and loving us completely, despite our flaws.

Side B: Friends are our musical directors.

They help us to orchestrate the music in our lives, the rhythm of our steps, the lilt in our voices and the melody of our laughter.

Leader: Jesus is our director, leading our souls in song, knowing the rhythm of our hearts and answering the notes of our questions with codas of true resolution.

Side A: Friends are our shoulders.

They allow us to lean on them when the weight of our worries and obligations seems too heavy. They support us in periods of hardship.

Leader: Jesus is our shoulder, sharing our burdens when we are overwhelmed and carrying us in times of need.

Side B: Friends are our light.

They ignite the fire of our smiles and laughter. They illuminate the darkness of the unknown with their companionship.

Leader: Jesus is our light, showing us the way of love and truth. He walks with us always.

Jesus is the true model of friendship: our healer, our mirror, our sounding board, our cheerleader, our microscope, our director, our shoulders and our light. We thank God for the gift of his Son, Jesus.
Amen.

Closing Reflection

God has given us the freedom to choose our friends. Friends are a reflection of us to the outside world, so we must choose them carefully. We need to be sure that our interests mesh and that together we can follow the same journeys of faith and truth. Successful friendships lead to inner and outer growth. Successful friendships garner inner contentment and happiness. Successful friendships give us a sense of belonging.

Closing Prayer

God of friendship,
thank you for the gift of your Son Jesus,
our truest friend.
May we always remember that when we share our burdens, they become lighter,
that true friendship tempers the bad in life and accentuates the good,
that joy shared with your Son grows even brighter,
and that love reflected in the face of Jesus makes our lives worth living.
+ Amen.

Closing Ritual

As true friends, let us share a sign of peace.

Make Time for God

*You shall love the Lord your God
with all your heart,
and with all your soul,
and with all your might.*

(Deuteronomy 6:5)

Introduction

As we go through our busy days, how many of us take a moment to pause and make time for God? Spending time with God brings growth of the spirit. Our souls are renewed when we pause each day and let God into our thoughts and hearts. This inner transformation strengthens our faith. Today's prayer service focuses on the importance of making time for God in our daily lives.

Opening Prayer

+ Loving Jesus,
while you lived on earth,
you made time for God.
You prayed on your own
and with others.
The stillness allowed you
to hear God's call
and to follow God's guidance.

Today, we ask you to help us
make time for God,
just as you did.
Let us open our eyes and hearts
so we can hear the word of God
and rejoice.
Amen.

Scripture: Colossians 3:15-17

Litany: Making Time for God

Leader: The Bible is rich with lessons and teachings that describe how making time for God transforms and renews our lives.

Reader 1: "I will always guide you and satisfy you with good things...."
(Isaiah 58:11)

Reader 2: Lord, you ask us to make time to listen to your word, which guides us and brings us closer to your love.
All: We hear God's guidance when we make time for God.

Reader 1: "He strengthens those who are weak and tired. But those who trust in the Lord for help will find their strength renewed. They will rise on wings like eagles; they will run and not get weary; they will walk and not grow weak." (Isaiah 40:29, 31)

Reader 2: Lord, you ask us to trust you when we are weary. You give us strength when we need it the most.
All: Our strength is renewed when we make time for God.

Reader 1: "The Lord is near. Do not be anxious about anything, but in everything, by prayer and petition, with thanksgiving, present your requests to God. And the peace of God, which transcends all understanding, will guard your hearts and your minds in Christ Jesus." (Philippians 4:5-7)

Reader 2: Lord, you ask us to pray during times of fear or worry.
All: Our hearts fill with courage when we make time for God.

Reader 1: "Trust in the Lord with all your heart … Remember the Lord in everything you do, and the Lord will show you the right way." (Proverbs 3:5-6)

Reader 2: Lord, you are beside us when we need comfort.
All: God comforts us during difficult times in our lives when we make time for God.

Reader 1: "[A]ll who find safety in God will rejoice; they can always sing for joy. Protect those who love God; because of God, they are truly happy." (Psalm 5:11)

Reader 2: Lord, you ask us to give thanks and to rejoice in your spirit.
All: We find true joy and happiness when we make time for God.
Amen.

Reflection

Invite participants to answer the reflection questions below using a paper and pencil. Allow a minute or two after each question.

- How do you make time for God at this point in your life?
- What can you do to increase your time with God?

Closing Prayer

Loving God,
it is you who
guides us,
grounds us
and protects us.
May we be ever thankful
for the gift of your love.
Give us the courage
to answer your call.
Remind us that there is renewal
in the silence and in the stillness.
May we always turn our hearts to you.
We ask this through your Son, Jesus.
+ Amen.

Coming Home: Reconciliation

Return to the Lord, your God,
for he is gracious and merciful,
slow to anger,
and abounding in steadfast love.

(*Joel* 2:13)

Opening Prayer

+ Loving God,
may we look to our hearts and find true
sorrow for our wrongdoings.
May we look to our fellow students for
understanding when we make mistakes.
May we look to our friends and family for
forbearance and patience when we slip up.
And may we look to you for your abundant
and loving forgiveness.
We ask this through your Son Jesus.
Amen.

Scripture: Luke 15:11-32

Litany: Coming Home

Leader: God of All,
when we sin and we are truly sorry,
**All: O Lord, we pray that you know
we are coming home to you.**
Leader: When we need understanding from
those around us,
**All: O Lord, we pray that you know
we are coming home to you.**
Leader: When we need to repent and to
cleanse our hearts,
**All: O Lord, we pray that you know
we are coming home to you.**
Leader: When we need to mend our
relationships,
**All: O Lord, we pray that you know
we are coming home to you.**

Leader: When we need to fix the
brokenness,
**All: O Lord, we pray that you know
we are coming home to you.**
Leader: When we need to prove our
faithfulness,
**All: O Lord, we pray that you know
we are coming home to you.**

Leader: Home is where we can rest,
knowing we are safe.
Home is the place of love, comfort and
acceptance.
Home should be where we can go with
open hearts and have our sins forgiven.
We are at home in your Son Jesus Christ.
**All: O Lord, we pray that you know
we are coming home to you.**

Leader: We know that you will make ready
for us, for we are coming home.
Amen.

Closing Prayer

Forgiving God,
you know us better
than we know ourselves.
You know our very essence,
our motivations, our fears,
our deepest thoughts.
We thank you for always greeting us with
open arms, though at times we go astray.
May we be guided by the example of your
loving Son Jesus Christ.
We know that you are always waiting for us.
For you know that we are coming home.
+ Amen.

Abide in My Love: Working Together

A threefold cord is not quickly broken.
(Ecclesiastes 4:12)

Opening Prayer

+ God of wisdom,
you call us together as a community.
Jesus tells us that wherever two or three of
us are gathered together, he is with us.
Let all of us here today share with others
the grace and love and justice that we
receive from you.
Your grace reaches out so we can reach out
to each other.
You warm us with your love so we can be
warm to each other.
Your justice calls us to virtue so we can be
virtuous with each other.
Bless this gathering and walk with us
all the days of our lives.
Amen.

Scripture: John 15:1-11

Litany: The Fruits of the Holy Spirit

Loving God,
you tell us that we abide in your love
and we can only bear the best fruit
if we are connected to you.
You hold our community together.
You give us purpose and vision.

Where there is division and harshness,
All: Let us teach love.
When gloom and despair rule,
All: Let us show joy.
When we find conflict and anger,
All: Let us bring peace.

Into our hurried lives,
All: Let us bring patience.
To those who have been neglected,
All: Let us offer kindness.
To those who have little,
All: Let us act with generosity.
In a world where connections to Christ can
be scorned,
All: Let us give witness by our faithfulness.
Among those who have been treated with
harshness,
All: Let us be your gentleness.
Into a world full of temptations and
distractions,
All: Let us model self-control.
Amen.

Closing Prayer

Loving God,
bless us and guide us.
Let us see your vision more clearly.
Let us open ourselves to your loving.
Let us practise those virtues
you have taught us.
Although we are all different,
teach us to live in harmony with each other.
Teach us to be gifts to our world.
May our community bless other
communities with your love.
We make this prayer in the name of Jesus,
the true vine.
+ Amen.

March

We Believe: The Tenets of Our Faith

I know the one in whom I have put my trust.
(2 Timothy 1:12)

Introduction

+ It is important to stand up for what we believe in. In this world, there are many different peoples, many different beliefs and many different faiths. Although we are so varied, we are all cherished children of God. God did not make us all the same. At Mass, we pray the Apostles' Creed and reaffirm the tenets of our faith. It is our calling to live up to our beliefs. We believe!

Scripture: Romans 1:16-17

Litany: We Believe

Leader: At Mass, when we pray the Apostles' Creed, we are stating the tenets of our faith and expressing what we truly believe. Praying the creed is a beautiful way to convey our faith.

I believe in God, the Father almighty, Creator of heaven and earth.
All: **We affirm our faith in God the Father, who gave us life, love, laughter.**
We believe.

Leader: And in Jesus Christ, his only Son, our Lord.
All: **We revere Jesus Christ our Lord and Saviour, man made flesh.**
We believe.

Leader: Who was conceived by the Holy Spirit
All: **We worship the Holy Spirit, God the Father and God the Son, our Triune God.**
We believe.

Leader: Born of the Virgin Mary
All: **We honour Mary, the mother of Jesus and our holy mother.**
We believe.

Leader: Suffered under Pontius Pilate, was crucified, died and was buried.
All: **We praise Jesus for his sacrifice of love for us.**
We believe.

Leader: He descended into hell; on the third day he rose again from the dead;
All: **We glorify God for the miracle of his Son's resurrection.**
We believe.

Leader: He ascended into heaven, and is seated at the right hand of God the Father almighty.
All: **We are in awe of the wonder of the Ascension.**
We believe.

Leader: From there he will come to judge the living and the dead.
All: **We pray that we may be judged worthy to live in the kingdom of heaven.**
We believe.

Leader: I believe in the Holy Spirit, the holy catholic Church…
All: **We are thankful for the gifts of the Holy Spirit. We are devoted to our faith.**
We believe.

Leader: The communion of saints…
All: **We depend on the constant intercession of the saints.**
We believe.

Leader: The forgiveness of sins…
All: **We humbly beg forgiveness for our transgressions.**
We believe.

Leader: The resurrection of the body, and life everlasting.
All: **We pray that we will join you in heaven and dwell in your holy presence forever.**
We believe.

Leader: Amen.
All: **So be it according to your divine will.**
We believe.
Amen.

Closing Prayer

All-powerful God,
you have made us in your image
and given us the gift of life.
You have created a bountiful world for us to live in.
You lovingly watch over us and walk with us daily.
You forgive us our sins and guide us on the right path.
You accept our prayers of thanksgiving and praise.
We glorify and honour your name.
May we be worthy to one day dwell with you in heaven.
For we believe!
+ Amen.

Lent 1: Prayer

To you I pray. O Lord ... you hear my voice.
(Psalm 5:2-3)

Introduction

+ When we speak to Jesus in prayer, we walk hand in hand with him and he shows us his love as he gently guides us along our faith journey. When we pray, we grow in faith and love. During the Lenten season, we are called to pray often. At all times, we pray in praise and worship and in thanksgiving for all our blessings. But during Lent, we are especially asked to look closely and honestly at ourselves and see if any of our outlooks or behaviours need to change. We pray during Lent for forgiveness for any wrongs we may have done.

Too often we are worried about what others think of us. We look for outside approval for our actions. Let us follow the example of Jesus and pray often.

Scripture: Psalm 20:4-6, 9

Litany: We Pray to You, Lord Jesus

All: We pray to you, Lord Jesus, for forgiveness
For the wrongs we have done
For the unkind words we have said
For the hurtful actions we have carried out

All: We pray to you, Lord Jesus, for understanding
Of the intentions of our hearts
Of our motives and meanings
Of who we are with all our failings

All: We pray to you, Lord Jesus, for guidance
To show us new directions and possibilities
To lead us away from negative lures
To direct us on how to cleanse our hearts

All: We pray to you, Lord Jesus, in praise
For your awe and majesty
For your unending love
For your ultimate sacrifice

All: We pray to you, Lord Jesus, in thanksgiving
For our talents and abilities
For our homes, our families, our friends
For our lives and the blessings we have been showered with

All: We pray to you, Lord Jesus, in worship
For your love for us despite our imperfections
For your patience with us even when we sin
For your faith in us that we will return to you

All: We pray to you, Lord Jesus, for strength
To stay the course you have set for us
To avoid the near occasion of sin
To walk with you each and every day.
Amen.

Closing Prayer

God of glory,
may our earnest prayers reach you in heaven
as we appeal for forgiveness, understanding, guidance and strength
and pray to you in praise, thanksgiving and worship.
We ask this through your Son Jesus Christ.
+ Amen.

Lent 2: Fasting

"Sin is lurking at the door; its desire is for you, but you must master it."

(Genesis 4:7)

Introduction

+ The season of Lent is a time for sacrifice and a time to resist temptation. We give up something that we like or give up a negative behaviour as a reminder that Jesus sacrificed his life for us on the cross. And just as Jesus resisted the temptations of Satan in the desert for 40 days, we are asked to resist temptation during the 40 days of Lent. Lent gives us the spiritual opportunity to follow in the footsteps of Christ.

Scripture: Matthew 4:1-11

Litany: Lead Us in the Footsteps of Christ

Leader 1: All-knowing God,
though we may hide our failings from others around us, we know that you see all. You call us to do our best to do what is right.

Leader 2: We know you understand that it can be difficult for us to resist temptation. Guide us along the right path to you. We pray…
All: **All-knowing God, lead us in the footsteps of Christ.**

Leader 1: God of sacrifice,
It's so difficult to give up something we like for the 40 days of Lent. Giving up a negative behaviour is hard, too. How can we do it? Who will know if we don't follow through?

Leader 2: Though our sacrifices seem big to us, they do not compare to the ultimate sacrifice Jesus made for us. Help us to persevere throughout these 40 days. We pray…

All: **God of sacrifice, lead us in the footsteps of Christ.**

Leader 1: God of fairness,
we may have been tempted to cheat on a test by looking at a neighbour's work, or to change the position of the ball in a game when no one was watching, or to say nothing when we were given too much change at the store.

Leader 2: These sins mark our hearts and taint our consciences. Help us to be honest and true to ourselves and others. We pray…
All: **God of fairness, lead us in the footsteps of Christ.**

Leader 1: When we are tempted by evil, or when we seek to hide our failings or find spiritual weakness within ourselves,

Leader 2: Let us take strength in following Jesus our guide, during this Lenten season and always.
All: **Lead us not into temptation, but deliver us from evil and lead us in the footsteps of Christ. Amen.**

Let us pray in the words that Jesus our guide and brother taught us:
Our Father…

Closing Prayer
God of love,
for 40 days, Jesus was tempted,
yet he did not give in
to the demands placed on him.
May we, too, persevere
throughout the 40 days of Lent
to find the salvation of Christ awaiting us.
Amen.

Lent 3: Almsgiving

For you were called to freedom,
brothers and sisters;
only do not use your freedom
as an opportunity for self-indulgence,
but through love become slaves
to one another.

(Galatians 5:13)

Invitation to Prayer

The season of Lent is the time for almsgiving. We are asked to share generously with those in need, so we can truly appreciate all the blessings that God has bestowed on us. Our gifts can be varied. We can offer our time or money. We can give of our talents or skills. We can share our love or prayers. The season of Lent gives us the spiritual opportunity to change and grow. Let us begin our prayer now with the sign of the cross. +

Scripture: Matthew 6:1-4

Litany: Almsgiving

All: May our offerings bring happiness and peace to others and joy to our hearts.
Let us give of our time. Let us bring our smiles, our conversation and our company to the lonely, the friendless and the ostracized. A visit or a phone call or sharing a cup of tea takes only a few moments, but can mean the world to someone who is alone.
All: Let us give our time.

All: May our offerings bring happiness and peace to others and joy to our hearts.
Let us share our talents and skills. Some have the gift of song; others, the gift of speech; still others have carpentry or cooking skills. When we share our gifts, we can bring delight to those around us.
All: Let us share our talents and skills.

All: May our offerings bring happiness and peace to others and joy to our hearts.
Let us donate money to help the poor. We cannot always directly reach all those in need, both within and outside our community, but many agencies can effect big changes in the lives of people in need. Our combined donations can purchase goods and services that result in dignity and hope for those who receive them.
All: Let us donate money to help the poor.

All: May our offerings bring happiness and peace to others and joy to our hearts.
Let us contribute our service. We can use our arms to sort clothing for those who need something to wear, our hands to work in a soup kitchen to feed the hungry, or our feet to walk in inner-city neighbourhoods, distributing blankets to those without shelter. Our efforts allow others to enjoy the basic necessities of life that we often take for granted.
All: Let us contribute our service.

All: May our offerings bring happiness and peace to others and joy to our hearts.
Let us offer our prayers. God hears every cry for help, every voice of supplication, every whisper for answers, every joyous laugh and every word of praise. Let us join our voices in the call to speak to our Lord in prayer. For everything good begins and ends with God.
All: Let us offer our prayers.
Amen.

Closing Prayer

Generous God,
may we share generously
with those less fortunate than us.
In our efforts, help us to answer the call to
be servants like Jesus.
Let us follow his example to
feed the hungry,
include those who are seeking
companionship,
clothe the poor, and
share our many blessings and gifts
with all.
For it is in serving and in giving in your
name
that we find the true meaning of life.
+ Amen.

Accepting the Challenge

"I am with you always,
to the end of the age."
(Matthew 28:20)

Opening Prayer

+ God of all hope,
disturb our complacency.
Push us to love even more.
Push us to forgive even more.
Push us to reach out even more.
Push us to listen even more.
Push us to seek eternal life even more.
Challenge us to make our schools and
homes places of justice and goodness.
Amen.

Scripture: Matthew 19:10-22

Gospel Meditation

The rich young man wanted to know the
way to eternal life. When we approach Jesus
in prayer, what do we ask of him?

Inside all of us, loving guide,
there is a rich young man
who is eager for your wisdom
yet afraid of your challenge.
Dear Jesus, meet us where we are.
Understand our needs and longings,
our fears and frailties,
our gifts and dreams.
But challenge us to go further:
to move from understanding your words to
living out your words.

Take us to those shores of possibility.
Teach us to go out into the deep,
to give away all that stops us from truly
loving.

Lead us to the mountaintop
to teach us again the law of love.
Walk with us through the halls of this school,
giving us warmth in our welcomes and
strength for the hard times.

Litany: Challenge

Loving God,
stretch our hearts and minds.
All: Encourage us and challenge us
To reach out to a heartbroken friend.
All: Encourage us and challenge us
To listen to the voices of the ignored.
All: Encourage us and challenge us
To stand up against injustices.
All: Encourage us and challenge us
To call ourselves Christians when it is
unfashionable.
All: Encourage us and challenge us
To pray to you faithfully and worship you
openly.
Amen.

Closing Prayer

God of challenge and compassion,
be with us in our questioning and doubts,
surround our fears with your love,
surround our despair with your hope,
surround our anger with your peace.
Lead us forward towards the boundaries of
our abilities
and then let us have the wisdom to follow
you to go beyond ourselves.
Bless our journey together.
We ask this in the name of Jesus
the challenger.
+ **Amen.**

The Need for Perseverance

My beloved, be steadfast, immovable.
(1 Corinthians 15:58)

Introduction

Today's prayer service focuses on the virtue of perseverance in our lives. Perseverance is continuing to do something in spite of difficulty or obstacles, and refusing to give up. Perseverance is a necessity of life that helps us grow closer to God. The Bible is filled with stories about people who were determined to keep to their course of action despite obstacles along the way.

Opening Prayer

+ Loving God,
as your faithful people,
we call to you
and place ourselves in your loving care.
We ask you to guide us and bring us comfort
as we face challenging times in our lives.
Help us to anchor our faith
in your word and in your wisdom.
Guide our thoughts and actions
so we may persevere
and grow closer to you.
Amen.

Scripture: James 1:2-5

Scripture Reflection

Sometimes it seems like no one understands what we are feeling in the midst of difficult situations. This scripture reading reminds us that God is always present, always merciful and understanding. During the most challenging moments in our lives, we are faced with a choice: to continue on or to give up. When we choose to persevere, we learn through our trials and tribulations. We are reminded that our faith gives us strength and endurance. Our spirits can only get stronger, bolder and braver when we allow ourselves to experience God within us.

Litany

God of love,
All: We pray for faith to persevere.

God of wisdom,
All: We pray for courage to persevere.

God of fortitude,
All: We pray for strength to persevere.

God of counsel,
All: We pray for guidance to persevere.

God of peace,
All: We pray for hope to persevere.

God of wisdom,
All: We pray for insight to persevere.

God of grace,
All: We pray for your presence in us to persevere.
Amen.

Closing Prayer

Let us close with the words that Jesus taught us.
Our Father…
+ Amen.

April

The Journey of Love: The Stations of the Cross

For in Christ Jesus … the only thing that counts is faith working through love.

(Galatians 5:6)

Opening Prayer

+ Loving Jesus,
in your unending devotion to us,
you have shown
gracious fortitude on your difficult journey,
serenity in the face of diversity, and
infinite patience and love to all around you.
Through your ultimate sacrifice,
you have granted us salvation.
As we journey through our lives,
may your peace speak to our hearts.
May we learn the value of tolerance and
compassion from your merciful example.
And may we walk with you to the gates of
heaven.
Amen.

Scripture: Acts 8:32-33

Leader: The First Station: Jesus is condemned by Pontius Pilate

Reader 1: You know that despite your being blameless, the road you must now travel will be long and difficult. You accept your fate with resolution and begin your journey of love.

All: Let us journey even when we know that the path will be long and arduous. May we find strength in the knowledge that Jesus will be with us for the duration of the journey. Let us walk with Jesus on his journey of love.

Leader: The Second Station: Jesus takes up the cross

Reader 2: The journey has just begun and you already feel the crushing weight of the heavy cross you have been made to carry. Yet your resolve does not falter and you do not object as you journey with love.

All: Let us walk with Jesus when life's burdens are placed upon us. May we find peace in the knowledge that he will help us to bear the load. Let us walk with Jesus on his journey of love.

Leader: The Third Station: Jesus falls for the first time

Reader 1: The heavy cross taxes your body. You fall under its weight. Yet you are still filled with resolve on your journey of love.

All: Let us walk with Jesus when our steps falter and when we fail. May we know that he will always help us to get up and continue. Let us walk with Jesus on his journey of love.

Leader: The Fourth Station: Jesus meets his mother

Reader 2: You meet your grieving mother. She weeps to see your suffering. You comfort her despite your pain as you continue your journey of love.

All: Let us walk with Jesus when our loved ones weep for us. May we be thankful that he will mourn with us and support us in our grief. Let us walk with Jesus on his journey of love.

Leader: The Fifth Station: Simon of Cyrene carries the cross

Reader 1: *Simon helps you. He bears the weight of the heavy cross for a while. Even though you did not ask for his help, you are grateful to him just the same as you continue your journey of love.*

All: Let us walk with Jesus when we need to seek help from others around us. May we not be afraid to ask for their assistance. Let us walk with Jesus on his journey of love.

Leader: The Sixth Station: Veronica wipes the face of Jesus

Reader 2: *The strain of bearing the cross makes you sweat. Veronica's gift is to wipe your face and cool your brow as you continue your journey of love.*

All: Let us walk with Jesus when we stop to appreciate the gifts that others share with us. May we value and graciously accept all gifts offered to us, whether small or large. Let us walk with Jesus on his journey of love.

Leader: The Seventh Station: Jesus falls the second time

Reader 1: *The weight of the cross becomes almost too much to bear. You fall a second time. You get but a few moments' respite from the heavy burden, then you continue on this difficult journey of love.*

All: Let us walk with Jesus even when we fail and feel that it is too difficult to keep going. It is at such times that we grow the most. May we allow the Spirit to give us the strength we need to persevere. Let us walk with Jesus on his journey of love.

Leader: The Eighth Station: Jesus meets the women of Jerusalem

Reader 2: *You meet the women of Jerusalem. They weep for you, yet you pray for them and tell them not to worry as you resume your journey of love.*

All: Let us walk with Jesus when we need the emotional support of friends and family. May we remain on our set course and continue in his love even when we need the encouragement of others. Let us walk with Jesus on his journey of love.

Leader: The Ninth Station: Jesus falls the third time

Reader 1: *The crushing weight of the cross causes you to fall a third time. It is even more difficult to get up. The cross continues to cut into your flesh, yet you will continue on this journey of love.*

All: Let us persevere even when we feel that it is just too difficult to go on. May we remember to draw strength from our Lord's example and to always love, even when we believe we cannot get up again. Let us walk with Jesus on his journey of love.

Leader: The Tenth Station: Jesus is stripped of his garments

Reader 2: *Your captors strip you and cast lots for your clothing, yet you are not swayed from your journey of love.*

All: Let us walk with the Lord even when others seek to strip us of our dignity. May we learn to bear the blows to our self-worth with grace, as Jesus did. Let us walk with Jesus on his journey of love.

Leader: The Eleventh Station: Jesus is nailed to the cross

Reader 1: *The soldiers brutally nail your hands and feet to the cross, causing you agonizing and searing pain. They have no regard for your pain. They laugh at you and taunt you, yet you are resolved to remain on your journey of love.*

All: Let us walk with Jesus even when we are persecuted, laughed at or treated badly. May we show more empathy for those who cross our life's paths. Let us walk with Jesus on his journey of love.

Leader: The Twelfth Station: Jesus dies

Reader 2: You die on the cross. Yet you do not blame those who have crucified you. You have journeyed with love.

All: Let us walk with Jesus even in the face of death. May we follow in the way of the Lord. Let us walk with Jesus in his journey of love.

Leader: The Thirteenth Station: The body of Jesus is removed from the cross

Reader 1: Your sacred body is taken down from the cross. You have been killed by those who know not what they have done. You have journeyed with love.

All: Let us walk with Jesus even when we feel that we have lost our battles. May we feel the warmth of his love in our hearts. Let us walk with Jesus on his journey of love.

Leader: The Fourteenth Station: Jesus is laid in the tomb

Reader 2: Your body is prepared and then laid to rest in a tomb. A large stone is rolled in front of the entrance to keep your body safe. You have journeyed with love.

All: Let us walk with Jesus even when we feel that the journey is over. May we rest in the knowledge that his ultimate sacrifice of love has opened the doors of heaven to us. Let us walk with Jesus on his journey of love.

Closing Prayer

Compassionate God,
we thank your holy Son Jesus,
who has travelled this difficult road
for us.
Help us in all our journeys to you.
May we maintain our resolve,
our direction and our faith.
For we know that the destination
will be worth it.
Let us walk in love with the Lord.
We ask this through your Son, our Lord and Saviour Jesus Christ.
+ Amen.

With Reverent Hearts

Happy are the people ... who walk, O Lord,
in the light of your countenance;
they exult in your name all day long,
and extol your righteousness.

(Psalm 89:15-16)

Opening Prayer

+ God of glory,
with reverent hearts we adore you.
With solemn praise we glorify you.
With sincere prayers we honour you.
May our words of worship reach you
on your holy altar in heaven.
We ask this through your Son,
Jesus Christ.
Amen.

Scripture: Malachi 2:4-7

Litany: With Reverent Hearts

Side A: Our reverence directs us to praise the word of God.

Side B: May our prayers resonate with echoes of your holy name.

All: Let us praise you with reverent hearts.

Side A: Our reverence inspires us to honour God's precious gift of life.

Side B: May we walk in faith in all we say and do.

All: Let us praise you with reverent hearts.

Side A: Our reverence binds us together as the family of God.

Side B: May we offer our grateful thanks for your love as your cherished children.

All: Let us praise you with reverent hearts.

Side A: Our reverence allows us to celebrate the wondrous blessing of creation.

Side B: May we offer you prayers of veneration for all the wonders of our world.

All: Let us praise you with reverent hearts.

Side A: Our reverence is a reflection of the Holy Spirit at work in us.

Side B: May we use this gift to express our adoration.

All: Let us praise you with reverent hearts.

Side A: Our reverence reveals the awe and wonder in our souls.

Side B: May our adoration show us the true way in you.

**All: Let us praise you with reverent hearts.
Amen.**

Closing Prayer

God of glory,
you are ever sacred,
ever blessed,
ever loved,
ever holy.
Accept our words of earnest praise.
We offer them to you with humble and reverent hearts.
+ Amen.

Easter Glory

"He has been raised; he is not here."
(Mark 16:6)

Opening Prayer

+ Jesus our risen Lord,
you have conquered death and opened
the gates of heaven for us.
You lead us from the darkness of sin
to the light of new life in you.
Let our hearts be open
to hear your words of salvation.
Amen.

Scripture: Matthew 28:1-10

Litany: Praise to the Lord

Lord of life,
we view the empty tomb with wonder,
for our Lord has conquered death and risen
to new life.
All: Praise to the Lord, who has risen in
glory.

Lord of light,
we view the empty tomb with faith,
for our Lord has banished the darkness
of the unknown and his holy light of
friendship shines on us all.
All: Praise to the Lord, who has risen in
glory.

Lord of love,
we view the empty tomb with joy,
for our Lord has left the unkind cold behind
and brings loving warmth to our hearts.
All: Praise to the Lord, who has risen in
glory.

Lord of hope,
we view the empty tomb with devotion,
for our Lord has delivered us from the
emptiness of false promises to the fullness of
his hope of heaven.
All: Praise to the Lord, who has risen in
glory.

Lord of jubilation,
we view the empty tomb with awe,
for our Lord has turned our mourning
into rejoicing and jubilation.

All: Praise to the Lord, who has risen in
glory.

Lord of truth,
we view the empty tomb with certainty,
for our Lord has bought us new life,
holy light, everlasting love,
the fullness of hope and rejoicing
and jubilation to our hearts
with his great sacrifice.
May our mouths ever praise his name.
All: Praise to the Lord, who has risen in
glory.
Amen.

Closing Prayer

God our Father,
through his sacrifice,
your Son has brought us new life in you.
He illuminates the way to your kingdom
with his holy light.
He watches over us with love
and gives us the hope of salvation.
May we ever praise and glorify his name.
We ask this through Jesus Christ,
our Risen Lord.
+ Amen.

New Life in the Light of Christ

"Let there be light."

(Genesis 1:3)

Opening Prayer

+ God of the resurrection,
in this Easter season,
may your light shine among us
in a new way.
May it dispel darkness and guide us.
May it illuminate our path and guide us
when we are lost.
May the warmth of your light nurture our
souls,
now and forever.
Amen.

Scripture: John 8:12-13

Gospel Meditation

The Gospel of John calls Jesus the Light of
the World. We are called to reflect the light
of Jesus into the dark places in our world.

But where is this light, God?
At times, the world seems so dark.
We hear about war, disease, famine and
corruption.
Clouds of despair block the light.
We ask, "What happened to the light?
The light you created at Genesis,
Jesus who is the Light of the World,
the Easter light?"
Sometimes we are blind to this light.
But it shines, nevertheless.
It shines even when we can't see it.

We trust in this light
and when we are at our best,
we reflect this light.
Can we become more than a metaphor?
More than a mirror of Christ's light?

Litany: Christ's Light

Let people see Christ's light in us.
When we stand up for the homeless,
All: Let Christ's light shine in us.
When we walk with the lonely,
All: Let Christ's light shine in us.
When we bring joy to our families,
All: Let Christ's light shine in us.
When we pray,
All: Let Christ's light shine in us.
When we seek to learn about creation,
All: Let Christ's light shine in us.
Amen.

Closing Prayer

May this Easter season be a time
when we again see your brilliance.
May we see through the clouds
the warmth of your light.
May we be bathed in Easter light
so that we can reflect it for each other.
May the light of Christ bring healing
and hope to our families, our school,
our community and our world.
We make this prayer
in the light of Christ's love.
+ **Amen.**

Walk with Me: Student Mentoring

Teach me the way I should go.
(Psalm 143:8)

Introduction

+ Being a student mentor means taking the hand of those you serve as guide, tutor, counsellor and friend. The task can be onerous at times, but rewarding. It is a big responsibility, not to be taken lightly. God has given us a wonderful role model to follow: Jesus is our mentor in all we do.

Scripture: Matthew 7:13-14

Litany: Walk with Me

Jesus, you are our mentor for life.
You lead us, advise us and guide us.
You invite us to walk with you every day.
And you say to us:
All: Walk with me
When you are lonely
and I will keep you company.
All: Walk with me
When you are restless
and I will give you ease.
All: Walk with me
When you are stressed
and I will offer you serenity.
All: Walk with me
When you stumble
and I will give you support.
All: Walk with me
When you need a friend
and I will listen to your heart.
All: Walk with me
When you need guidance
and I will lead you.

All: Walk with me
When you are distressed
and I will give you comfort.
All: Walk with me
When you are sad
and I will mourn with you.
All: Walk with me
When you are content
and I will share in your happiness.
All: Walk with me
When you are weak
and I will give you strength.
All: Walk with me
When you are afraid
and I will not leave your side.
All: Walk with me
When you are ill
and I will pray with you.
All: Walk with me
When you do not understand
and I will open your eyes.
All: Walk with me
When you are embarrassed
and I will love you just the same.
All: Walk with me always
and I will show you my love.
Jesus our friend, guide and mentor,
we will walk with you.
Amen.

Closing Prayer

Jesus our mentor,
guide us through our life's journey.
Lead us to salvation in you.
Counsel us when we stray
Teach us to follow the true path.
+ Amen.

Living in Harmony with the Earth

*A harvest of righteousness is sown in peace
for those who make peace.*

(James 3:18)

Introduction

+ Our world's natural resources are being used up faster than we can renew them. Yet as the global population increases, so does our pillaging of the earth. We are called to take good care of this planet, for it was created by God and is the only home we have.

Opening Prayer

God of the earth,
you have given us abundant resources to sustain us.
Teach us to use these gifts with faithfulness, generosity and wisdom.
We ask this through your Son Jesus Christ.
Amen.

Scripture: Philippians 4:4-9

Litany: Living in Harmony

May we use the world's resources we need with love, humility and deference to others, without guilt, without fear, without waste.
All: May we live in harmony with the earth.

May we live in balance with the wildlife with which we share this planet, without needless harm to them or to their ecosystems.
All: May we live in harmony with the earth.

May we respect the life in our lakes, rivers and oceans, using them with care and being conscientious in our efforts not to pollute these valuable resources.
All: May we live in harmony with the earth.

May we learn to reduce our excesses and continue our efforts to reuse and recycle all we can so that little is wasted.
All: May we live in harmony with the earth.

May we plan to leave the world in a state that all future generations will be able to enjoy a bountiful and healthy planet home filled with abundant diversity and enough resources for all to use and enjoy.
All: May we live in harmony with the earth.
Amen.

Let us pray in the words Jesus our brother taught us:
Our Father…

Closing Prayer

God of harmony,
we look to your Son to guide us
in our human existence.
We look to follow his instruction.
May we emulate his promise.
We ask this through Jesus, your Son, our brother and friend.
+ Amen.

May

Maintaining Morality in a Broken World

*Surely goodness and mercy shall follow me
all the days of my life.*

(*Psalm 23:6*)

Introduction

In our media-filled world, there never seems to be much in the way of good news. Headlines are often filled with stories of crime, brewing political battles and war, as well as natural disasters such as earthquakes and tornadoes. Good news items always seem to find their way to the back of the newspaper, the bottom of the web page, or the last few minutes of the TV or radio news. Why don't we value the good news as much as we value the bad?

Even during our leisure time, we watch movies and TV shows that contain storylines geared to make money and increase viewer numbers but do not truly mimic real life. Sometimes we try to emulate the behaviours we see on the big and small screens, forgetting that we are viewing paid actors and not real life. Why is it hard to see that our morality in real life should be different from what we watch in our leisure time?

How do we maintain morality in a broken world?

Invitation to Prayer

Our expectations of life can be skewed by what we hear and see in the media. We become desensitized to negativity. We become disappointed when we don't dress like, look like and act like the stars we see on TV. We experience brokenness in our relationships. Our world is a broken one, but it can be mended. Let us open our prayer service in the name of the Father, and of the Son, and of the Holy Spirit. + Amen.

Scripture: Galatians 5:22-25

Litany: Mending Our Broken World

Our world is broken in some ways, but we can mend it together.

All: Let us mend our broken world and build heaven on earth.
When ethics can seem like a suggestion, let us earnestly seek the higher moral ground. In our effort to reach it, we will become better people, for it is in making the attempt that we grow closer to God.

All: Let us mend our broken world and build heaven on earth.
Where virtue and honour can appear to be undervalued, let us hold them aloft for all to see and make them the rule, not the exception. The rewards that await us are worth the effort.

All: Let us mend our broken world and build heaven on earth.
Where common decency is not ostensibly extolled, let us strive for respectability and courteous behaviour every day. For these are the signposts leading to heaven.

All: Let us mend our broken world and build heaven on earth.
Where integrity is not the norm, let us set high, principled standards and listen to the

sound advice of our conscience, for it is there that Jesus whispers to us.

All: Let us mend our broken world and build heaven on earth.
Above all, let us follow Jesus as our guide. With him walking beside us, we will never lose our way, for he is the true conduit to finding heaven on earth.

All: Let us mend our broken world and build heaven on earth by earnestly seeking out high moral ground, making virtue and honour the rule, striving for respectability, and listening to our conscience.

Let us mend our broken world and build heaven on earth by following the true way with Jesus. Amen.

Reflection

Keep your eyes focused on the life of Jesus. Pray often. It doesn't have to be in a formal setting or always with others. It doesn't have to be in a ritual or in song. It can be these things, too, but they are not requirements. Just talk to God every day, in quiet moments. Allow the Holy Spirit to gently infuse you with good intentions, good values and good leadership. Know that God is good! Know that Jesus died for you because you're worth it! Know that your life is better with Jesus as your guide.

Closing Prayer

Glorious God,
help us to recognize that
what we see in the media
is not necessarily the way
we should live.
Guide us in the right path
that leads to happiness in you.
Help us to appreciate and internalize
the truth of your goodness and light,
for only then can we set about to repair this broken world.
Only then can we begin to make heaven on earth.
We ask this through your Son, our Lord and guide, Jesus Christ.
+ Amen.

Closing Ritual

Let us now offer each other the sign of peace.

In Praise of Mothers

* Dedicated to our mothers
and those who have mothered us in our past,
mother us in our present and
will mother us in the future. *

Those who respect their mother
are like those who lay up treasure.

(*Sirach* 3:4)

Introduction

+ Before we took our first breath,
we were known by our mothers.
They felt our hearts beating,
our bodies moving and our legs kicking.
Some of us were chosen after we were born,
to become part of another loving family by
mothers who cared for us and loved us.
Our mothers held our tiny fingers and
kissed our sleeping forms.
They bathed us, clothed us, fed us,
nurtured us… loved us.
Some of us found a special person to mother
us and guide us through the storms of life.
We thank God for our mothers.

Scripture: Proverbs 31:25-31

Litany: In Praise of Mothers

All: Let us praise all mothers
As they rejoice in our successes,
no matter how small.
All: Let us praise all mothers
As they care for us when we are sick.
All: Let us praise all mothers
As they support us and
bolster our spirits when we fall.
All: Let us praise all mothers
As they mourn with us when we are sad.

All: Let us praise all mothers
As they worry about us.
All: Let us praise all mothers
As they forgive our failings.
All: Let us praise all mothers
As they encourage us in all we do.
All: Let us praise all mothers
As they pray for us every day.
All: Let us praise all mothers
As they exult, rejoice, care, teach, support,
mourn, worry, forgive, encourage and pray
for us…
As they love us.
All: Let us praise all mothers
As they teach us how to love
unconditionally by example.
Thank you, God, for mothers.
Amen.
Let us now pray to Mary,
the mother of Jesus:
Hail Mary…

Closing Prayer

God of love,
we thank you for the gift of our mothers:
mothers to labour to bring us into this
world,
mothers to guide us on our life's journey,
mothers to teach us how to pray to you.

We praise you, God,
for our mothers who listen to us and cry
with us,
who applaud our progress and laugh with us,
who want the best for us, who dream with us,
who love us always.
We thank you, God,
for the gift of our mothers.
+ Amen.

Into the Deep: Questioning Within – Discernment

Now faith is the assurance of things hoped for,
the conviction of things not seen.
(Hebrews 11:1)

Introduction

As Christians, we are called to be discerning believers – to have faith and full confidence in God's truth. Faith is not something we can see. It is something we feel with the heart, for it is in our hearts that God dwells. Today's prayer service helps us to explore our faith journey.

Opening Prayer

+ Loving God,
you call us to be
discerning believers.
Open our eyes and ears
to your teachings about faith.
When we pray,
you answer.
When we seek you,
you are there.
And yet there are times
when we doubt.
Strengthen our faith
so that we may follow your word.
Remind us, O Lord,
that you are always there for us,
and that we live in your constant love.
Amen.

Scripture: Luke 5:1-11

Scripture Reflection: A Shared Reading

Reader 1: How do you think the fishermen felt when Jesus told them to put their nets deep into the water for a catch?

Reader 2: At first, we didn't understand what Jesus wanted us to do. We had been fishing all night, and our nets were empty. We know how to fish… we just didn't have any luck finding fish that night.

Reader 1: And yet, the fishermen took the risk and followed what Jesus had asked them to do. They had to trust Jesus. They had to cast their fears aside and let go. Let go of all reason and take a leap of faith. They did what Jesus asked them to do. They pushed their nets into the deep water and waited…

Reader 2: And then it happened… a miracle right before our eyes! At first we were afraid of what might happen. But we found comfort in the words that Jesus said: "Don't be afraid…" And then we weren't. We trusted the Lord. The next thing we knew, our nets could barely hold all the fish we caught!

Reader 1: Jesus asks us, too, to cast our nets of faith deep into the sea and live our lives with faith in our hearts. Our faith guides us, strengthens us, and fills us with hope. Every act of faith brings us closer to God's love.

Closing Prayer

God of faith,
throughout his life on earth,
your Son Jesus brought light and glory
to people everywhere.
As your discerning believers,
you call us to have trust in you,
to cast our nets deep into our faith,
to leave the comfortable and the familiar
and just trust you.
Help us to stand firm in our faith
and remain steadfast in the Holy Spirit
so we may live in your grace forever.
+ Amen.

A Vision of Grace

From his fullness we have all received,
grace upon grace.

(*John 1:16*)

Invitation to Prayer

+ Too often we are caught up in our busy lives. We worry about completing all the tasks we set for ourselves. They may seem important, but they distract us from seeing simple wonders and mundane miracles of everyday life. May we see that no matter how small or seemingly inconsequential or commonplace, each blessing around us is a vision of grace.

Scripture: James 1:17-18

Litany: A Vision of Grace

God has given us a world filled with all that we need to thrive and grow. Let us recognize that every blessing is a vision of grace.

In the food we eat, whether a gourmet meal, a quick lunch or a simple piece of bread. It nourishes us, sustains us, helps us grow and saps our hunger.
All: Let us recognize that every blessing is a vision of grace.

In the fluid we drink, whether a hot drink on a cold day, a cool cup of juice or a simple glass of water. It comforts us and quenches our thirst.
All: Let us recognize that every blessing is a vision of grace.

In the places we live and grow: our homes, our schools, our churches. They shelter us, protect us, keep us safe and provide centres for community education and faith.
All: Let us recognize that every blessing is a vision of grace.

In the beauty of the sky, whether it is moonlight to guide us, starlight to wish upon or sunlight to bask in, the light warms us and allows us to dream.
All: Let us recognize that every blessing is a vision of grace.

In those who share our lives, whether friends, family, acquaintances, neighbours or strangers. They offer us company and love. They teach us, support us and pray with us.
All: Let us recognize that every blessing is a vision of grace.

In the variety of gifts we all have and share with others, whether they are gifts of song, writing, sport, caring, laughter or love. They enlighten our spirits, elate our hearts and brighten our souls.
All: Let us recognize that every blessing is a vision of grace.
Amen.

Closing Prayer

God of grace,
may we be thankful
for all the gifts you bestow upon us.
May we always recognize and delight in all visions of grace.
We make this prayer in the name of Jesus.
+ Amen.

Called to Ministry: A Marian Prayer Service

Then Mary said,
"Here am I, the servant of the Lord;
let it be with me according to your word."

(Luke 1:38)

Opening Prayer

+ Mary, holy Mother,
you are the Mother of Jesus:
caring, strong and faithful.
Be with us when God calls us
to serve others.
so that we may follow your example of
determination, conviction and devotion.
For you are ever blessed by God.
Amen.

Scripture: John 2:1-11

Litany: Mary Is Our Model

Mary, pure of heart, mind and body,
accepted the Angel Gabriel's news that she
had been chosen to bear the Son of God.
Her deep faith in God told her that this was
the right thing to do. Yet this decision was
not one to be taken lightly, for Mary was
betrothed to be married. She would have to
tell Joseph of her resolve.
All: Mary is our model of faith.
May we follow her example
when we are called to serve.

Mary, pure and faithful, knew she would
have to face the community with her news.
Even though she knew the reaction would
not be a positive one, Mary accepted the
responsibility of becoming the Mother of
Jesus. Her great inner strength allowed her
to withstand the criticism.

All: Mary is our model of strength.
May we follow her example
when we are called to serve.

Mary, pure, faithful and strong, fled with
Joseph to Egypt to protect her newborn
son from Herod's soldiers. Though she was
afraid, her resolve was not shaken. She
willingly embraced her lifelong mission of
caring for her son, Jesus. Her unconditional
promise to serve God and protect his Son
would solidify her determination.
All: Mary is our model of service.
May we follow her example
when we are called to serve.

Mary, pure, faithful, strong and willing to
serve, encouraged Jesus to perform his first
miracle at the wedding in Cana. She knew
he would begin his ministry. She knew that
her abundant love for her Son would stay
with him, no matter where he went.
All: Mary is our model of love.
May we follow her example
when we are called to serve.

At the foot of the cross, Mary's heart was
breaking, for her beloved son was to die.
Her deep faith, great strength, abundant
love and unconditional promise to serve
God would carry her through the next few
days. These elements of leadership have
made Mary our model of leadership and
ministry.
All: Mary is our model of leadership.
May we follow her example
when we are called to serve.
Amen.

We pray that, like Mary, we will answer the call to ministry when we hear God's voice. May Blessed Mary continue to bless us with her presence.

Let us pray together to our holy Mother:

Hail Mary…

Closing Reflection

Mary, though young and afraid, was steadfast in her resolve to bear the Son of God. Despite the challenges she faced, she remained firm in her ministry. May we learn from her, our holy Mother, what it means to be willing to serve, to have deep faith, to love intensely, and to find inner strength. May we, too, show these qualities when we hear God calling us to serve.

+ Amen.

One Kind Word

Do not lag in zeal, be ardent in spirit,
serve the Lord.

(Romans 12:11)

Introduction

+ It is our task to continually move forward on our faith journeys. As long as we strive to move along, we can be assured of our place in heaven one day. We should begin each day knowing that we'll do something good. We can do a good deed or accept the gift someone else bestows on us. We can learn a new lesson or pass on our knowledge to another. But through all of these actions, we are called to take what we are and evolve into something even better than when we began. It is our responsibility to develop, grow and become. God wants us to use his gifts by serving him.

Scripture: 1 Peter 1:5-7, 10-11

Litany: One Kind Word

All it takes is one kind word to begin.
All: One kind word
Leads to one friendly smile.
All: One friendly smile
Becomes one thoughtful gesture.
All: One thoughtful gesture
Grows into one good turn.
All: One good turn
Leads to one noble deed.
All: One noble deed
Changes to one useful morning.
All: One useful morning
Becomes one great act of service.

All: One great act of service
Progresses into one worthwhile day.
All: One worthwhile day
Leads into one evening's prayer of thanksgiving.
All: One evening prayer
Takes us into one good night's rest.
All: One good night's rest
Leads to one earnest morning prayer of praise.
All: One earnest morning prayer
Begins one regular routine.
All: One regular routine
Matures into one good life.
All: One good life
Leads us to the one true God in heaven. And all it took to begin
was one kind word.
Amen.

Closing Reflection

God gives each of us varied skills and gifts in order to build his kingdom on earth. It is our responsibility to take our God-given potential and run with it. With these abilities, we provide the energy and the willpower to advance and progress. We mustn't waste our precious gifts. We need to take responsibility to make them grow even more beautiful every day.

What kind word will you begin your day with?
+ **Amen.**

June

Walk the Talk

"In everything do to others
as you would have them do to you."
(Matthew 7:12)

Opening Prayer

+ Loving God,
you created us and know us better
than we know ourselves.
We ask for your grace and courage to
always be ourselves.
Our lives are both struggles and gifts.
Bless us with patience and wisdom in our
struggles.
Help us to share our gifts with others.
Help us to sort voices of goodness from
voices of temptation.
Help us to nurture our best selves.
Help us so we may help friend and stranger
alike.
Amen.

Scripture: Luke 10:25-37

Gospel Meditation: The Path to My Truest Self

In the parable of the Good Samaritan,
Jesus challenges the boundaries of our love.
Who is beyond our caring? Can we truly be
people of faith and neglect those who are
different from us? If we are to walk the road
between Jerusalem and Jericho, do we walk
not only with eyes of faith but also help
those along the road who need our help?

*

Sometimes it feels easier to close my eyes
and walk on.

I live such a busy life, a rushed life.
I promised my friends I'd be with them.
And I can't stop.
I tell myself that there'll be others who can
help.
But you, loving God, see beyond my
excuses and into my deepest self.
You know my fears, my weaknesses,
my struggles, my doubts, my joys, my loves
and my triumphs.
Help me to always be my true self,
not the self of excuses and shallow
attachments.
Help me to be my true self
with my friends, in the classroom,
and at the dinner table.
Our world tells us that we are what we wear
or what we eat,
and that pleasure, prestige and security are
the supreme values.
But we know that there is another path:
the path of giving to others,
of humility and love.
This is our true path.
Lead us there to our true home with you.

Litany: Our Lives Are Pilgrimages

Our lives are pilgrimages towards
ever deeper love.
We know that we were meant for love, but
there are so many unloving obstacles in our
paths.

Lead us from selfishness and self-absorption.
All: Guide us and sustain us.
Lead us from prejudice and fear.
All: Guide us and sustain us.

Lead us from despair and cynicism.
All: Guide us and sustain us.
Lead us from easy answers and
narrow-mindedness.
All: Guide us and sustain us.
Lead us from hypocrisy and deceit.
All: Guide us and sustain us.
Lead us from lies and omissions.
All: Guide us and sustain us.
Lead us to truth and insight.
All: Guide us and sustain us.
Lead us to harmony and hospitality.
All: Guide us and sustain us.
Lead us to hope and joy.
All: Guide us and sustain us.
Lead us to understanding and wisdom.
All: Guide us and sustain us.
Lead us to wonder and awe.
All: Guide us and sustain us.
Lead us to honesty and integrity.
All: Guide us and sustain us.
Amen.

Closing Prayer

God of justice,
open our hearts to those around us
who are hurting and wounded.
Cleanse our hearts of jealousy and
prejudice.
Help us to bring healing and hope
to our families, our school, our community
and the world.
We ask for this strength through Jesus
the teacher and healer.
+ Amen.

We Belong Together

A friend loves at all times.
(Proverbs 17:17)

Opening Prayer

+ God, our loving friend,
bless our community.
We are grateful for your guidance
along the roads we have taken together.
Continue to watch over us and lead us.
Open our ears to hear your words this day
and always.
Amen.

Scripture: Acts 2:43-47

Scripture Meditation: Friendships Aren't Easy

If only that community in the early Church
were our community.
It seems so idyllic.
Friends with a common purpose,
a common vision and a common belief.
But that's not us.
That's not the way we are.
When I listen to my friends,
we talk about who is upset
or who is going off the rails.
We are anxious about what we will do
when we leave school.
If truth be told, we are scared of what others
think about us.
If my friends and family really knew who I
was, would they still love me?
Into this insecurity, I invite my faith.
Only with you, God, can I find my resting
place, my place of peace, my true home.
You are my anchor.

You are my centre point
when relationship storms wash over me.
You give me a purpose and a vision and belief.
From this strong centre,
I reach out to my friends.
Loving God, be my guide in this search.

Litany: Bless Our Friendships

Loving God,
bless our circles of friendships
in this place and in our homes and
communities.
In our learning and our working,
All: Bless our friendships.
In our brokenness and our healing,
All: Bless our friendships.
Amid our fighting and our forgiving,
All: Bless our friendships.
In our talking and our listening,
All: Bless our friendships.
In our yearning and our dreaming,
All: Bless our friendships.
In our arriving and our departing,
All: Bless our friendships.
Amen.

Closing Prayer

Loving God,
you invited us to be your friend and family.
May our hearts always be open to your love
and guidance.
Teach us to be good friends
to each other and to you.
Bless our relationships
with peace and joy,
this day and always.
We pray in your compassionate name.
+ Amen.

Dare to Dream

*"What no eye has seen, nor ear has heard,
nor the human heart conceived,
what God has prepared
for those who love him."*

(1 Corinthians 2:9)

Introduction

+ Dare to dream… dream big! Know that you can achieve just about anything you truly set your heart on by following three constant tenets: faith in God, faith in yourself, and faithful dedication to achieving your goals. God sees the potential that each of his children is born with. It is up to us to stretch our imaginations, broaden our horizons, widen our scope and reach for our dreams.

Scripture: Jeremiah 29:11-14

Litany: Dare to Dream

All: Dare to dream. Have faith in Jesus as your guide.
Allow Jesus to guide your footsteps
and have bearing on all your decisions
and you will be set on the right path.
When you walk with him,
believing in you,
how can you doubt your own abilities?
Dare to dream. Have faith.

All: Dare to dream. Have faith in yourself.
Broaden your horizons.
Look beyond your immediate comfort zone.
Have confidence in your own abilities.
Dare to dream. Have faith.

All: Dare to dream. Have faith in your dedication.
Work hard towards your goals so you can achieve them.

Don't settle for the mundane. Be a doer.
Dare to dream. Have faith.

All: Dare to dream. Have faith in God.
Above all, have faith in God.
Stretch your imagination and picture what you could become,
what you could do,
how you could affect the world
and what legacy you could leave behind.
God sees all that you can be
and envisions the possibilities.
Allow yourself the freedom to imagine,
to see, to believe.
Dare to dream. Have faith.

All: Dare to dream.
Follow Jesus, believe in yourself,
dedicate your efforts to success
and trust in God's wisdom.
Dare to dream big.
Dare to dream in colour.
Dare to dream in faith.
Dare to dream.
Amen.

Closing Prayer

God of dreams,
we know that what we will be in life
is in your hands.
We are limited only by our whims,
by the scope of our imaginations,
and by the work we put into achieving our goals.
Lead us. Teach us. Guide us.
May we find our way in you.
May we dare to dream.
+ Amen.

Looking Back in Gratitude

I give thanks to my God always for you.
(*1 Corinthians 1:4*)

Opening Prayer

+ Creator God,
thank you for the gift of life.
Open our minds and hearts
so we may give to you
the only appropriate response
to such generosity:
deep, abiding gratitude.
For it is in continuous thanksgiving
and rejoicing
that we draw closer to your love.
Amen.

Scripture: 1 Thessalonians 1:2-7

Scriptural Meditation

St. Paul begins his letter to the Christians in Thessalonica, Greece by thanking them for their faith, love, good works and hope. We also look back with gratitude on our school community this year.

*

We get stuck thinking about our troubles.
We can think of ourselves as victims.
God calls us to go beyond self-pity
into the realm of gratitude.
Like St. Paul,
may we rejoice in our friendships
and even our hardships.
St. Paul saw hardships as gifts that showed him the power of hope and resilience.
Even our difficulties can help us to grow.
You've heard it said "No pain, no gain."
That could also be said of our spiritual life.

From our pains, we can make spiritual gains.
From our heartbreak, we find within us the power of forgiveness.
From disputes, we can find compassion to see others' points of view.
For both hardships and joys, we are grateful.

Litany: We Are Grateful

For friends and teachers,
All: We are grateful.
For family and leaders,
All: We are grateful.
For our school and community,
All: We are grateful.
For our parish and diocese,
All: We are grateful.
For our beautiful yet broken world,
All: We are grateful.
For laughter and conversation,
All: We are grateful.
For silence and peace,
All: We are grateful.
For joy and hope,
All: We are grateful.
Amen.

Closing Prayer

Gracious God,
you welcome us into your world
of beauty and grandeur.
May we reflect your goodness in our
daily lives with an attitude of gratitude.
Keep our hearts warm and open.
May your grace flow into our places of
worship, learning, resting, working and
playing.
We ask this through Christ our Lord.
+ Amen.

Graduation

Commit your work to the Lord,
and your plans will be established.

(Proverbs 16:3)

Opening Prayer

+ Loving God,
today we come together
to celebrate the end of a chapter
for our graduating class.
Thank you for your presence
in their lives.
Thank you for allowing them to share
their gifts
with the rest of the world.
Continue to help our graduates
to grow in love and wisdom.
Be near them and guide them
in all their adventures.
May they continue to be blessed
in all they do, today and always.
Amen.

Scripture: 1 Timothy 4:6-12

Prayers of Petition

For each petition, the response is:
Lord, hear our prayer.

For the world's leaders, called to make
decisions with the future of the youth in
mind and God's love in their hearts.
We pray to the Lord.
All: Lord, hear our prayer.

For ongoing support and guidance from our
families. We pray to the Lord.
All: Lord, hear our prayer.

For the friendships we have formed at
school, sustained by God's everlasting love.
We pray to the Lord.
All: Lord, hear our prayer.

For our graduates who are moving on, as
they experience joys and challenges in the
next chapter in their lives. Fill them with
strength and guidance, and illuminate their
paths with your love always.
We pray to the Lord.
All: Lord, hear our prayer.

For all of us gathered here today,
as we venture into the summer in faith,
surrounded by God's love.
We pray to the Lord.
All: Lord, hear our prayer.

Loving God,
listen to our prayers
and send us your Holy Spirit
to guide and protect us always.
Amen.

Closing Prayer

Gracious God,
bless our graduates
as they go forward into the future.
Remind them that the past is done
and that all they have
is the journey ahead of them.
Illuminate their path
with your everlasting light.
Guide them
so that each step they take
is a step closer to your love.
We ask this through your Son
Jesus Christ our Lord.
+ Amen.

Journeying into Summer

Lead lives worthy of the Lord,
fully pleasing to him,
as you bear fruit in every good work.
(*Colossians 1:10*)

Opening Prayer

+ God of our journey,
as we move on
to new adventures this summer,
we thank you for walking with us this year.
May we continue the journey with you by
our side.
We ask this through Jesus our Lord.
Amen.

Scripture: 2 Samuel 22:29, 31-34, 36, 37

Litany: Guide Us

Jesus our leader,
direct us today so that we may follow you
always.
Show us the way to your Father's kingdom.
Guide us in your footsteps.

All: Guide us to possibility and opportunity,
For we know that new experiences,
new obligations and new challenges await
us.

All: Guide us to determination and achievement,
For we know that we will be called to exert
our best efforts to master new tasks.

All: Guide us to faith and confidence,
For we know that you will erase all doubts
and fears over the coming months.

All: Guide us to truth and love,
For we know that it is through our
expression of these that we enrich our
hearts.

All: Guide us to meaning and answers,
For we know that it is in the search that we
learn the most about ourselves.

All: Guide us to generosity and kindness,
For we know that it is in demonstrating
these building blocks of life that we
enhance our communities.

All: Guide us to peace and serenity,
For we know that it is only in you that we
can experience true harmony and find true
rest.

All: Guide us to understanding and conviction,
For we know that it is in our earnest prayers
that we open our hearts to new learning.
Amen.

Closing Prayer

Compassionate God,
teach us to show gentleness and peace
from within our hearts,
generosity and love in our actions,
and reverence and wonder in our prayers.
May we grow in faith as we walk with you
by our side.
And may we speak the words for the
journey that resound with your
devotion, wisdom, compassion and
harmony.
We ask this through your Son Jesus Christ
our Lord.
+ Amen.

Appendix: Preparations and Rituals

This section gives suggestions for prayer focal points and rituals you may wish to include in your prayer services. If you use the prayer service during a different liturgical season than the one suggested in the book, simply change the coloured cloths to suit the liturgical season or occasion. For all prayer services, explain to all participants beforehand how the prayer, particularly the rituals, will unfold, in order to preserve the sacred atmosphere.

Before the prayer service:

❖ Hand out copies of the prayer service.

❖ Set up the liturgical focal point. Consider including the following items:

- o A cloth in the appropriate liturgical colour
- o Candles (votive, pillar or tea lights)
- o Crucifix
- o Bible
- o Picture or symbol of the school's patron
- o Rosary.

❖ Select the readers.

❖ Arrange the seating.

❖ Explain any ritual actions that might take place.

September

1. Beginning the Journey: A New School Year

Place a green cloth for Ordinary Time, a bible and a lit candle on the prayer focal point. You could also include items associated with school, such as books, laptop, pencils, protractor, ruler, etc.

2. Let Your Voice Be Heard

Place a green cloth, a bible and a lit candle on the prayer centre. Consider adding symbols of home, school, church and community.

3. Take Heart, Take Courage

In the prayer focal point, place a lit candle, a bible and a green cloth. You may also add symbols of fall, such as leaves, corn and brightly coloured gourds.

4. The Light of Insight

For the prayer focal point, include a bible, a green cloth and symbols of learning, such as books, binders, pens, a globe, lab instruments. The most important focal point will be a lit candle, which is referred to throughout the prayer service.

5. Leadership Matters: Student Government

Place a green cloth, a lit candle and a bible on the prayer table. You may wish to include symbols of student leadership in your school.

6. Who Is Jesus?

On the prayer table, place a green cloth, a lit candle, a cross and an open bible. You may also wish to include icons or pictures of Jesus.

October

1. We Belong: School Teams and Clubs

On the prayer centre, place a green cloth and a bible. You may wish to add some equipment or symbols of your school's teams and clubs.

2. Being Thankful

Place a green cloth, a cross, a lit candle and a bible on the prayer table. Add Thanksgiving symbols and decorations.

3. Let the Light Shine

Place a green cloth and nine small candles around a larger lit candle on the prayer focal point. As each part of the litany is read, after the phrase "Let the light shine" is spoken, light one small candle from the larger one.

4. The Virtue of Compassion

Place a lit candle and a tablecloth on your prayer table. As students arrive, hand out a pencil and piece of paper so they can think about the scripture reflection and discuss responses if desired. You may also wish to include pictures of people who are symbols of compassion, such as Mother Teresa, the pope, various saints and the school patron.

5. Called to Witness

Consider adding pictures or icons of the figures mentioned in the litany to your prayer focal point.

6. Living Our Faith

On the prayer centre, place a green cloth, a bible and a lit candle. Consider including representations of various school social justice endeavours.

November

1. Teach Us to Love: All Saints' Day

Add a green cloth and a bible to the prayer centre. You may also add pictures or icons of the patron saint of your school or any of the people mentioned in the prayer service.

2. We Look to You: All Souls' Day

On the prayer focal point, place a green cloth, a lit candle and a bible. You may also include pictures of loved ones who have died.

3. Turning the Wheels of Justice

Place a green cloth, a bible and a lit candle on the prayer table. If space permits, have students stand in a circle to represent the united wheel of justice.

4. All Are Welcome: Equality and Acceptance

Students should surround the prayer focal point. A circle represents all being equal, since it has no place that is set apart. On the prayer centre, place a green cloth, a bible and a cross. Decorate with pictures of people of different ages, ethnic backgrounds, genders, physical and developmental abilities, etc.

5. Instruments of Peace: Remembrance Day

On the prayer table, place a red tablecloth, poppies and a cross. Light a red pillar candle. You may also wish to include a copy of a Remembrance Day book, such as *In Flanders Fields*. Consider playing "The Last Post" and end the two minutes of silence with "O Canada."

6. Healing a Broken World: Social Justice

Arrange students in a circle to signify unity and harmony. Place a cross, an open bible and a lit candle on the prayer table.

December

1. Advent 1: Waiting in Hope

On the prayer table, place a purple cloth for Advent and an Advent wreath. Assign a student to light the first candle.

2. Advent 2: Waiting in Faith

On the prayer table, place a purple cloth and an Advent wreath. Assign a student to light the first two candles.

3. Advent 3: Waiting in Joy

On the prayer table, place a purple cloth and an Advent wreath. Assign a student to light the first three candles.

4. Advent 4: Waiting in Love

On the prayer table, place a purple cloth and an Advent wreath. Assign a student to light all four candles.

5. Gifts for the Season

At the focal point include the Advent wreath, a Jesse tree, food, toys or clothing. Use a purple cloth for the Advent season.

6. Christmas Blessings

Place an Advent wreath on the prayer table and light the appropriate number of candles, depending on the week of Advent. Hand out pencils and paper to students and invite them to write down their responses to the scripture reflection questions. The shared reading may be acted out.

January

1. Nurturing the Soul

To set the mood, play some calming background music as students arrive. Place a lit candle and a tablecloth on the prayer focal point. Include a small bowl of mustard seeds, if possible.

2. Take Time to Pray

Place a green cloth for Ordinary Time, a lit candle and a cross on the prayer table. Add different representations of time, including a watch or clock, a timetable or calendar, a laptop.

3. Opening the Lines of Communication

On the prayer centre place a green cloth, a bible and a cross. You may also include different modes of communication, such as cell phone, laptop, letters, pictures of face-to-face communication, etc.

4. Bridges and Walls

This prayer service includes a story. Either use the script, assigning it to an accomplished reader, or ask someone to rehearse the story and tell it dramatically. Include pictures or models of bridges and walls in your prayer focal point. A topographic map and a compass can also be placed here.

5. St. Thomas Aquinas: God Directs Our Lives

Place a picture or icon of St. Thomas Aquinas on a green cloth at the prayer focal point. Add books and an open bible.

6. Trials: Exam Time

On the prayer focal point, place a green cloth and a cross. Around the cross place notebooks, textbooks, pencils and pens.

February

1. The Journey Continues

On the prayer table, place a white cloth (if the date falls before the Baptism of the Lord) or a green cloth (if the date falls after that feast day), a lit candle and a bible. You may wish to include a road map or other symbols of journeying.

2. The Key to Wisdom

Place a green cloth for Ordinary Time on the prayer table if the date falls before Ash Wednesday, or a purple cloth for Lent if it is after Ash Wednesday. Add a bible and a lit candle.

3. The True Model of Friendship

Place a green cloth on the prayer table if the date falls before Ash Wednesday or a purple cloth if it is after Ash Wednesday. Add a bible, a lit candle and pictures that denote friendship, such as holding hands, smiling faces, hands in prayer, someone crying on the shoulder of another, etc.

4. Make Time for God

To the prayer focal point, consider adding a cross and an open bible.

5. Coming Home: Reconciliation

Students can dramatize the Prodigal Son story for this prayer service. On the prayer table, add a purple cloth if it is Lent (along with other Lenten symbols, such as rocks, sand and ashes) or a green cloth if it is Ordinary Time. Add a bible and a lit candle.

6. Abide in My Love: Working Together

If this prayer service is held in Lent, use a purple cloth. Grapes or grapevine designs can be used.

March

1. We Believe: The Tenets of Our Faith

Use a purple cloth on your prayer focal centre. Add a lit candle and an open bible.

2. Lent 1: Prayer

Place a purple cloth, a lit candle and an open bible on the prayer table. Add Lenten symbols such as rocks, sand or ashes.

3. Lent 2: Fasting

Place a purple cloth and a lit candle on the prayer table. Add Lenten symbols such as rocks, sand or ashes.

4. Lent 3: Almsgiving

Place a purple cloth and a lit candle on the prayer table. Add Lenten symbols such as rocks, sand or ashes.

5. Accepting the Challenge

Create a "wordle" (see www.wordle.net) of the key words in this prayer service and use it as a poster in the prayer centre. Use a purple cloth for this Lenten prayer service.

6. The Need for Perseverance

Since this season is Lent, place a purple cloth and a large lit pillar candle on the prayer centre. You may also wish to invite each student to light a taper candle to signify God's everlasting presence throughout our lives.

April

1. The Journey of Love: The Stations of the Cross

Select students to act out each station as a silent tableau. This approach is effective when simple costumes and props are used. Students are to hold each pose in silence while the description is being read. Make sure that the transitions between stations are also silent.

2. With Reverent Hearts

If it is before Easter, use a purple cloth to decorate your prayer centre and add Lenten symbols such as rocks or sand. If it is after Easter, use a white cloth and Easter symbols, such as flowers. Add a lit candle.

3. Easter Glory

Place a white or gold cloth on the prayer table to signify Easter glory and majesty. Include Easter symbols such as lilies and lit candles.

4. New Life in the Light of Christ

Include Easter symbols such as lit candles, flowers and a white cloth in your prayer centre.

5. Walk with Me: Student Mentoring

Include different pictures or depictions of hands being held and hands folded in prayer. On the prayer table, include a white cloth, a bible and a lit candle.

6. Living in Harmony with the Earth

Include natural items such as rocks, plants and water, or pictures of nature, in the prayer centre. Add a bible and a lit candle.

May

1. Maintaining Morality in a Broken World

Place a green cloth on the prayer table. Add an open bible, a cross and a lit candle. You may also wish to include newspaper clippings, magazine articles or movie ads to symbolize morality in today's media.

2. In Praise of Mothers

On a green cloth (for Ordinary Time) on the prayer table (or a white cloth if it is the Easter season), place a bible and a basket. You may also wish to add Mother's Day cards to the decorations. As students enter, give them a cutout and a pencil. Ask them to write the name of their mother or someone who has been like a mother to them. Then ask them to place the cutout in a basket on the prayer table. The prayer service will be dedicated to their mothers.

3. Into the Deep: Questioning Within – Discernment

Place various symbols of our faith, such as a bible, a cross, a rosary and a lit candle, in the prayer centre. You may also wish to add a picture of the school's patron saint.

4. A Vision of Grace

Place a green cloth, a lit candle, a cross and a bible on the prayer table.

5. Called to Ministry: A Marian Prayer Service

Place a green cloth, a lit candle and a bible on the prayer table. Include pictures or icons of Mary.

6. One Kind Word

Place a green cloth, a lit candle, a cross and a bible on the prayer table. As students enter, hand them a strip of coloured construction paper and direct them to the prayer focal point, where they are to add their piece of paper as a link to others to make a paper chain.

June

1. Walk the Talk

Include symbols of a journey, such as a map, compass, walking stick, water bottle, guidebook, knapsack and first-aid kit in your prayer focal point. Before Pentecost, use a white cloth. After Pentecost, use a green cloth for Ordinary Time.

2. We Belong Together

Include symbols of friendship (pictures, circle of friends) and the school (mascot, banner, picture of patron) in your prayer focal point. Before Pentecost, use a white cloth. After Pentecost, use a green cloth.

3. Dare to Dream

Place a green cloth, a cross, a bible and a lit candle on the prayer table. Add pictures of the sky taken during the day and night.

4. Looking Back in Gratitude

Add posters or word sculptures with words such as *Thanks* and *Gratitude* to your prayer focal point. Before Pentecost, use a white cloth. After Pentecost, use a green cloth for Ordinary Time.

5. Graduation

The prayer focal point can include a scroll tied with ribbon, a graduation cap and other symbols that represent learning, such as books, placed on a green cloth. You may choose to raise your right hand over the graduates as a sign of blessing as the closing prayer is read aloud.

6. Journeying into Summer

Place a green cloth, a bible and a lit candle on the prayer table. Add symbols of summer: sunglasses, flip flops, a novel, a road map, a plastic pail and shovel, etc.